CONTRIBUTIONS
TO
ASIAN STUDIES

CONTRIBUTIONS TO ASIAN STUDIES

Editors: K. Ishwaran and Bardwell L. Smith

VOLUME 17

ISLAM IN LOCAL CONTEXTS

Edited by Richard C. Martin

LEIDEN
E. J. BRILL
1982

ISBN 90 04 06829 5

PRINTED IN THE NETHERLANDS

Contents

CONTRIBUTIONS TO ASIAN STUDIES SERIES

Despite socio-cultural, economic, political and geographical diversity, the countries of Asia display certain broad similarities. In general, all of them are products of ancient civilizations, faced with the complex forces of modernity, which they have responded to in quite complex ways. Asia's unity in diversity, the dynamics of its social and cultural patterns, past and present, have stimulated a large body of scholarly work. A new phase in Asian studies has developed through first rate contributions from indigenous scholars who often bring an outlook and understanding of their own. *Contributions to Asian Studies,* a semi-annual publication, is intended as a forum for scholarly analyses of Asian societies and cultures, past and contemporary, from the diverse standpoints of the international community of scholars in all the social sciences and humanities.

Preface

ISLAM IN LOCAL CONTEXTS as it is approached by most of the authors in this volume is not exactly congruous with either Islamic studies or Asian studies as these are usually discriminated within academe. Oriental studies and more recently Near and Middle Eastern "area" studies, the usual departmental designations of scholars working on Islamic material, are terms of insufficient scope and accuracy for the project at hand. Also, and perhaps conversely, because the underlying topic refers to Islamic social and cultural contexts, the inclusion of papers on the Middle East (West Asia) and Africa indicates that the field is here differently conceived than Asian studies as such. The operating assumption that runs through each of the papers is that Islam always and everywhere, like other religious traditions, exists in local cultural, historical, political and geographical contexts. The problems attending the description and interpretation of Islam in some of these far-flung contexts in which it has existed or presently exists is what each author has essayed in his or her paper.

Among scholars in anthropology, institutional and social history, history of religions and the humanities such ventures as the present one occasionally occur in multidisciplinaty (if not yet truly "interdisciplinary") formats: conferences and symposia, panels at professional associations and published anthologies. The idea of devoting an edition of *Contributions to Asian Studies* to Islamic topics originated among the editors of the journal. The event that brought this possibility into view was a panel on "Islam and Popular Religion" at the 1980 annual meeting of the American Academy of Religion in Dallas, November 5-9. The five presentations and the discussion that followed drew on scholarly interests that covered Asia, South Asia, the Middle East and Africa, crossing several religious traditions and academic disciplines. With encouragement from Associate Editor Bardwell Smith, it was decided to prepare a volume by calling for additional papers on the same theme. The shift from "popular" to "local" was a conceptual refinement that resulted from discussions by the panelists; the connotation of "popular" Islam as an abberation of the "true" Islam requires making certain assumptions that fewer specialists are willing to make in these kinds of studies, even though *sensu stricto* "popular" denotes that which is constituted and carried on by the people—a legitimate meaning of what these studies intend. The preferred term "local" is used by anthropologist Clifford Geertz and discussed by Dale F. Eickelman in the first paper.

Eickelman's paper answers the need a volume of this sort has of providing the reader with an orientation in some of the theoretical and applied research that informs many of the essays that follow. "The main challenge for the study of Islam in local contexts," Eickelman tells us, "is to describe and analyze how the universalistic principles of Islam have been realized in various social and historical contexts without representing Islam as a seamless essence on the one hand or as a plastic congeries of beliefs and practices on the other." Many of the rest of the papers are also addressed to these concerns as well as to the process of the Islamization of non-Muslim peoples and symbols and to other forms of cultural symbiosis involving Islamic and adjacent or socially intermingled non-Muslim groups, as well as the process of cultural change and transformation. The influence of such figures as anthropologist Clifford Geertz and historians Marshall G. S. Hodgson and Peter Brown appear explicitly and implicitly in many of the papers. More encouraging for the developing consensus in this kind of study, many of the contributors are familiar with and refer to each other's work in contexts outside of these papers.

While the majority of the papers are written from the perspectives of social science and the historical disciplines, the contributions by Annemarie Schimmel and Azim Nanji belong more to the humanities, demonstrating the rich resources that local oral and written art forms provide for this kind of study. Thus, the volume is introduced by an anthropologist reviewing a kind of academic concern that in the nature of things has received the most attention from social scientists. Yet most of the contributors are, by profession, social historians, humanists and historians of religions who have found common cause with those social scientists devoted to understanding the complex relationship between textual and contextual expressions of religion in local environments, and to investigating the process of cultural change and transformation.

It is a special pleasure to be able to include a paper on "The Qur'ān in China" by Dr. Jin Yijiu, of the Institute for Research on World Religions in Beijing, People's Republic of China. Dr. Jin presented a version of his paper at the International Association for the History of Religions in Winnipeg, Canada in August 1980, and the original Chinese version of his paper was recently published in Beijing. It goes without saying that the work of Dr. Jin and his colleagues will be of considerable interest to scholars outside of China; opportunities for exchanges and cooperation in research will surely prove to be of enormous value to the academic community at large.

Without requiring a substantial contribution to the academic theme of this volume, the editorial responsibility has been nonetheless demanding. Consistency in transliteration within each paper was set as the highest priority and, to a large extent among the several papers, a common editorial style has been implemented. The technical terms and proper names, coming as they do from numerous Asian, South Asian and Middle Eastern languages, were standardized as much as possible. The *pinyin* system of Mandarin Chinese romanization, John T. Platts' *Dictionary of Urdu, Classical Hindi and English*, and the system of transliterating Arabic to English followed by most English language journals provided the main criteria. Complete accuracy has been qualified perhaps by the shortened time factor in producing a journal volume and by the fact that publisher, editors and contributors were spread out across several nations and continents in fixed or temporary locations, thus frustrating the process of consultation and proof reading.

I wish to acknowledge the generous and competent assistance of my colleagues at Arizona State University, Professor Timothy Wong of the Department of Foreign Languages and Professor Anne Feldhaus of the Department of Religious Studies; the matters alluded to above were rendered much easier by their help, especially in checking for accuracy and consistency in Chinese and Sanskrit transliterations. I should also like to thank Professor Bardwell Smith of Carleton College who arranged for the publication of these papers in *Contributions to Asian Studies*. Most of all I am indebted to each of the nine authors whose enthusiasm for and efforts toward this project made this work possible. It is a personal pleasure to be associated with their contributions to the study of Islam in local contexts.

Richard C. Martin

Arizona State University
Tempe, Arizona, U.S.A.

Contributions to Asian Studies, Vol. XVII

The Study of Islam in Local Contexts*

DALE F. EICKELMAN
New York University, New York, N.Y., U.S.A.

> A text is imbedded in specific historical time. ... To read fully is to restore all that one can of the immediacies of value and intent in which speech actually occurs.
> George Steiner, *After Babel*, p. 24

THE STUDY OF A WORLD RELIGION in local contexts implies what from some perspectives is obvious—any religion's ideology and practice are elaborated, understood and subsequently reproduced in particular places and at particular moments. Even eternal truths are necessarily revealed in a specific language and setting; for the instance at hand "in Arabic, that ye may be understood."[1] The notion of locality as represented here is now at least in principle a familiar part of the intellectual landscape of social historians and social anthropologists concerned with the study of Islam. Yet like any complex notion it has diverse ramifications and has developed in manifold, sometimes even incongruous ways. One scholar has recently gone so far as to suggest that the term *Islam* be replaced by *islams*, thus emphasizing the multiplicity of Islamic expression and asserting that in all historical and cultural contexts the *islams* of elite and nonelite, literate and illiterate, and theologians and peasants, are all equally valid expressions of fundamental, "unconscious" Islamic principles. The *islams* approach, inspired as a reaction both to the orientalist search for an ahistorical Islamic "essence" and to the somewhat parallel venture of neo-*tauḥîdî* or unitarian Muslim fundamentalists who regard their interpretations of Islam as definitive, ironically and unintentionally provides a conceptual endproduct which likewise reduces Islamic tradition to a single, essentialist set of principles.[2] It also disregards the fact that most Muslims quite consciously hold that their religion possesses central, normative tenets and that these tenets are essential to an understanding of Islamic belief and practice.

The main challenge for the study of Islam in local contexts is to describe and analyze how the universalistic principles of Islam have been realized in various social and historical contexts without representing Islam as a seamless essence on the one hand or as a plastic congeries of beliefs and practices on the

* I wish to thank Karen I. Blu, Richard C. Martin, William R. Roff and Kenneth Sandbank for their constructive comments on an earlier version of this paper.

other. This essay seeks to assess major recent trends in the study of Islam in local contexts and suggests new directions for further research on the basis of recent scholarship.

Beginnings

The notion of local as recently developed is considerably more complex than earlier sharp distinctions between, for instance, the concept of "great" and "little" (or "folk") traditions introduced by anthropologists and historians in the late 1940s as a means of better describing large-scale civilizations such as those of China, India, and Islam. As initially employed, this conceptual distinction was a useful way of indicating the possible relationships between religious traditions as known through the texts and exegeses of literati on the one hand and religious expressions and interpretations in village or folk contexts on the other. Unlike the earlier doctrine of "survivals," which presumed that folk traditions were somehow vestiges of earlier civilizations and less permeable than "high culture" to change, the notion of great/little traditions made no gratuitous assumptions concerning the historical precedent of some civilizational elements over others. As the notion of great/little traditions first began to develop, it enabled scholars working primarily with texts and those working in "field" settings to see the complementarity of their interests and to reassess their working notions of text and context. Yet as ordinarily reported, these various forms of religious expression were often merely juxtaposed and were not used as a base for the analysis of their complex interrelationships. Some anthropologists and historians, for instance, derived notions of normative or "orthodox" Islam from the tenets of orientalist scholars and wrote of observed village practices or local documents as "deviant," or accepted without question similar interpretations by Muslim scholars. The notion of "local" in such instances carried the misleading implication of something provincial, or an inferior and imperfect realization of "genuine" or "high" culture religious belief and practice, as opposed to popular and "vulgar" ones.[3]

One of the more influential Islamic historians of the 1950s and 1960s to incorporate the notion of great and little traditions in an integral way into his own work was the late Marshall Hodgson. His explicit concern was with "high" culture in the "primary milieu of Islam," which to him was constantly renewed and transformed by the dialogues of successive generations of "piety-minded Muslims" with the formative ideals of their civilization. Hodgson acknowledged that the traditions of "peasants or even non-lettered peoples" share substantially the same dynamics of change, but he explicitly left aside any detailed description of such changes or how they may have been interrelated to those of the "high" culture.[4] As Edmund Burke III subsequently argued, Hodgson's notion of the dialogue of successive generations of "piety-minded Muslims" with Islam's formative ideals comes close to an essentialist vision of Islam which minimizes some aspects of historical context and which

Hodgson himself deplored in the work of other scholars.[5] Nonetheless, Hodgson constructed a history of Islamic civilization that unlike many others was not unduly centered upon the Arab Middle East and that depicted in detail the changing forms and contexts in which Islamic ideals were expressed. Moreover, the recognition at least in principle of such transformations occurring among peasants and the non-lettered was a major step in advance of many other historians of Islamic civilization.

If the problem of Islamic historians as exemplified by Hodgson has been how to relate the vicissitudes of high culture to the rest of society, anthropology's basic conceptual problem has been how to apply what ethnographers have learned from the study of religious practice in small-scale groups or communities to larger entities such as Islamic faith or civilization. Because the published work of Clifford Geertz now spans more than two decades and has had a pervasive influence on scholars of many disciplines, it provides the best point of departure for tracing shifts in how anthropologists have sought to contribute to the study of Islam. Three of his principal studies are considered here.[6]

Although Geertz modestly asserts that his principal goal in *The Religion of Java* (1960) is primarily descriptive, his text contains a set of theoretical assumptions concerning how to represent adequately the culture of a complex religious tradition not limited to a single regional or national setting.[7] Javanese religious beliefs and practices are divided into three principal "orientations" or "cultural types." The *abangan* is "broadly related to the peasant element of the population," the *santri* stresses the "purer" Islamic aspects of Javanese syncretism and is "generally related to the trading element," and the Hinduist *prijaji* tradition is related principally to the "bureaucratic" element of the population.[8] Geertz argues that these three "subtraditions" are refractions of an underlying cultural unity, so that for instance the *prijaji* and *abangan* cultural orientations are "in part but genteel and vulgar versions of one another."[9]

The "in part" caution in the last citation and the use in other contexts of qualifications such as "generally" and "broadly" in relating religious subtraditions to particular social categories suggest Geertz' awareness of the difficulties involved in adequately representing the subtraditional "strands" of Javanese religious belief in the context of cultural theory as it had developed through the 1950s. The title of the book itself, as opposed to alternative possibilities such as *Islam in Java* or some sort of parallel to Bellah's *Tokugawa Religion*, represents an implicit choice in how to depict Islam in a Javanese setting. When Geertz writes, perhaps ironically, that the holiday of *rijaja* is "a kind of master symbol for Javanese culture, as perhaps Christmas is for ours," and that if one understood "everything" concerning *rijaja*, "a simple impossibility—one could say one understood the Javanese," he appears to suggest reservations concerning the usefulness of the holistic notion of culture as a guide to ethnographic reporting, at least in complex cultural settings.[10]

Islam Observed (1968) makes two major conceptual contributions through its detailed comparison of religious belief and practice in two geographically antipodal Islamic settings. First, in discussing what analytic notions such as "mysticism" can mean in particular settings, Geertz suggests a strategy of comparison based upon "family resemblances" rather than upon typological classifications which presume in advance the essential features of phenomena being compared. The result is to depict in concrete instances how Islam can remain catholic to "an extraordinary variety of mentalities ... and still remain a specific and persuasive force with a shape and identity of its own.[11] Second, Geertz seeks to convey the historical context in which the dominant "classical" styles of Islam in Indonesia and Morocco developed and reached their full form, thus setting his work apart from cultural studies that attenuate historical concerns. As a consequence even Edward Said exempts Geertz from the condemnatory strictures which he applies to most other scholars and characterizes him as a scholar "whose interest in Islam is discrete and concrete enough to be animated by the specific societies and problems he studies."[12]

"Suq" (1979), although not intended principally as a discussion of religion, complements Geertz' earlier studies on Islam by describing in intricate and convincing detail the relationship between the institutional framework of the bazaar economy of Sefrou, Morocco, and local religious institutions. These were the religious lodges (*zāwiyas*) in which most urban traders and artisans participated, and the system of pious endowments (*ḥubus*; *waqf*) which were controlled in practice by the local trading community that in turn benefited most from it. This was in part because the commercial properties rented by pious endowments were generally offered below market value, thus serving as an indirect subsidy to the bazaar sector of the economy.[13] In "Suq" more than in Geertz' earlier studies, the practical articulation of religious ideologies and institutions with specific social classes and groups is made explicit. If in *The Religion of Java* religious "subtraditions" were "broadly" and "generally" correlated with particular social categories without any elaborate discussion, in "Suq" these interrelations are, in my judgment, more precisely documented.

Yet a paradox emerges from the ethnographic analysis in "Suq" which is also present to some degree in the earlier studies mentioned here. Geertz describes the shifting political and economic contexts in which Sefrou's bazaar economy has existed as meticulously as oral history and written sources allow. Despite the major political and economic changes that have occurred since 1900, he argues that the "cultural framework" for economic transactions "has altered but in detail."[14] Geertz carefully specifies that it is the cultural framework for economic transactions in the bazaar and, by implication anyway, not the "total" cultural framework that has hardly altered over the last eighty years. Yet in *Islam Observed* the argument is similarly weighted toward an elucidation of the more constant classical religious "themes" and "styles."

To my knowledge, Geertz' most thorough discussion of religious change occurs in a 1972 article, based upon a 1971 return visit to Java and Bali, which serves as a temporal extension and reconsideration of his earlier *Religion in*

Java.[15] In this article, which provides an explicit discussion of the 1965 coup and subsequent massacres, Geertz suggests that the most salient religious development has been the "hesitant" emergence of "something rather like a denominational pattern of religious organization or affiliation," toward a "more openly pluralistic system," if not always a tolerant one, composed of Islam, *kebatinan* (Javanese mysticism), Christianity, and Bali-Hinduism, in which there is a growing recognition that the Muslim community, "properly understood" (i.e., composed of exemplary purists), is a minority community in Java.[16] In spite of this growth of denominationalism, there is paradoxically—Geertz' term—a "convergence in religious content" as each denomination is becoming Indonesianized by "a turn toward a more experiential sort of faith, and especially toward mysticism," a trend which "has been a central characteristic of Javanese religiosity for centuries" and which constitutes an "underlying—*the* underlying—theme of Javanese ... religiosity: personal, inward, transcendental experience—a direct, personal confrontation with the numinous."[17] If cultural frameworks alter so little despite major political and economic shifts—the "great transformations" described by Marc Bloch in depicting the emergence of feudal society in Europe, Max Weber in analyzing the "iron cage" of modern industrial and bureaucratic society, or perhaps Clifford Geertz in discussing religious change in twentieth century Java—then a much more explicit theoretical discussion is needed of what is it in the nature of "cultural frameworks" that seemingly allow them to be transmitted and reproduced over time with relatively little change.

Class and the Social Reproduction of Religious Forms

In recent years there has been a shift in studies of culture or systems of meaning toward discerning how they are transmitted and reproduced, and how they shape and in turn are shaped by configurations of power and economic relations among groups and classes in different societies. Much more than in earlier studies, there is an effort to articulate specific economic, political and historical contexts with patterns of religious faith and experience. For some scholars, the writings of Max Weber have provided a useful point of departure in understanding changes in religious ideologies and institutional forms. Michael Gilsenan, for instance, used Weber's ideal typical notions of authority as a means of explaining why one Egyptian brotherhood was able to expand and maintain its membership at a time when other brotherhoods experienced apparently irreversible declines. Gilsenan suggested that the brotherhood, by adapting the patterns of bureaucratic authority characteristic, for instance, of the government office for which the order's founder worked, managed to solve leadership and organizational problems that plagued other brotherhoods. At the same time the brotherhood's emulation of "modern" organizational forms enhanced its status in the eyes of members and potential recruits.[18]

Studies that depict the debate in specific cultural contexts over *what* is Islam and *who* opts for particular interpretations of Islam are especially valuable for comprehending changes in how Islam is locally understood, even when such studies are not explicitly informed by theoretical problems. One of the most outstanding of such studies is the work of Ali Merad on the reform movement in Algeria.[19] He argues that reformist ideologies in the period from 1925 to 1940 essentially were educated urban interpretations of an "intelligible and simple" Islam made against the backdrop in Algeria of prevalent and nearly all-pervasive maraboutic interpretations of Islam tied to specific tribal and rural contexts. Unlike Hodgson, who merely assumes that both "high culture" and folk versions of Islam undergo change and renewal, Merad shows the intimate and necessary interrelationship between the religious understandings of the reformist elite and those of ordinary tribesmen and peasants. Although the conscious goal of reformist leaders was to reconstitute a more purist version of Islam in Algeria, Merad suggests that an indirect consequence of reformism was to popularize a "rationalist" conception of Islam which set religious doctrines and practice apart from other aspects of social life.[20] Similar linkages between elite and popular interpretations of Islam and their relations to social classes and status have been explored in other regions as well.[21]

A recent anthropological study that particularly seeks to explore the relation between religious ideology and class is Clive Kessler, *Islam and Politics in a Malay State* (1978). Kessler claims that he has methodologically tried to steer a dialectical middle passage between what he calls "idealist phenomenology," in which cultural symbols are analyzed and elaborated without significant reference to "nonideational elements," citing Clifford Geertz as an example, and an equally unsatisfactory "hard 'objectivism' that reduces all cultural phenomena to some underlying material or quantifiable base."[22] The only effective means of eliciting what Kessler precisely implies by his dialectical middle course is to follow his basic argument in detail.

Essentially he seeks to analyze the factors which contributed to the success in Kelantan of the Pan-Malayan Islamic Party (PMIP) from 1959 to 1969 in attracting a majority of peasants votes. Some prior analysts attributed the PMIP success simply to the "exploitation of religious sentiments for political objectives" or to "illicitly invoked religious slogans" that assume the existence of "irrational" religious sentiments. To demonstrate the weakness of such assumptions, Kessler elaborately describes the historical and social contexts in which the PMIP operated and what were the dominant religious sentiments in Kelantan at various times.[23]

For Weber, Islam is one of the few major world religions with an "essentially political character."[24] Kessler argues that the nature of Islam's political character has not been clearly understood. Despite the claims of some Muslims that Islam possesses a "perfect social theory," he argues that this theory is "sociologically deficient" because it primarily concerns individual ethics and ignores the presence of groups and classes. Its focus is upon how to motivate individuals, "initially governed by base and personal interests," by higher moral principles which enable them to transcend narrow self-interest. Even in "classical" Muslim society, the "idealistic, ethical, and individualistic" Islamic vision of a just society remained unrealized, so that there is almost inevitably "a tension between the social experience a believer seeks to apprehend and the terms his religion furnishes for its apprehension."[25]

Throughout his text Kessler rapidly shifts from writing about Islam to discussing Kelantanese Islam—an adjectivalized term used by him to emphasize the elaboration in a regional context of elite and popular notions of belief and practice. In this context the Islamic vision of a moral, ideal society is sustained principally if sporadically through the major collective rituals of Islam. Occasions such as the fast of Ramaḍān, which is shared equally by all Muslims and thus symbolizes the ideals of equality, harmony and disinterested motivation of all believers, enables them temporarily to discard all other social distinctions. It is a period in which the *akal* (reason [Arabic *ʿaql*]) of each believer informs him with the discipline necessary to overcome *nafsu* (passion and self-interest) and live a fuller life as a Muslim. Kelantanese Islam thus enables peasants "to fashion social action, and thus experience themselves, in a manner consonant not so much with formal and explicit Islamic social theory as with its implicit but often problematic terms."[26]

To explain how the PMIP became popularly identified with the Islamic vision of Kelantanese peasants, Kessler provides a convincing social history of the interrelationships between landownership, religion, and political action, and especially the various divisions which occurred among the traditional ruling elite. Although opposition political parties promised the peasant electorate that they would undertake concrete measures to improve peasant life if granted support, most nonetheless voted for the PMIP despite its lack of a practical platform to improve the lot of the peasants. The PMIP won peasant support because it articulated the Islamic vision of the just society, "consisting of individuals motivated by principle rather than immediate self-interest." Kessler argues that like fasting and the pilgrimage, elections entailed for most peasants a suspension of the normal social order. By claiming to be "implementing Islam," the PMIP identified itself with the exercise of *akal* and other Islamic ideals. By attacking the claims of the PMIP and asking peasants to consider their material conditions, the opposition became popularly associated with self-interest (*nafsu*) and against Islam. Since in making these judgments Kelantanese peasants were acting in terms which they generated themselves rather than those which others imposed upon them, an adequate explanation of the PMIP successes and the significance of "idealized Islamic notions of personal identity and social existence" long remained inaccessible to outsiders.[27]

Kessler's elegantly argued explanation of PMIP success inadvertently indicates how difficult it is to steer a middle course between presenting a political economy of the contexts in which religious beliefs and practices are developed and maintained, and describing how such beliefs serve (to paraphrase Kessler) as an idiom for apprehending social experience and shaping social action. The political economy component of Kessler's argument, detailing patterns of change in trade and landownership and their impact upon the Kelantanese elite and peasant society, is excellently presented, built as it is upon his own research and complementary monographs by social historians concerning the development of Malay nationalism and the growth of the Malay intelligentsia during the colonial period.[28]

Yet Kessler's account of how peasants actually apprehend their religion is largely inferential. In Chapter 11, "Religious Ideas and Social Reality," he uses extracts from the speeches of several political leaders and quotations from James Siegel's excellent presentation of key elements (including *akal* and *nafsu*) in the world view of Atjehnese Muslims.[29] Only once does Kessler quote the remarks of a "devout Kelantanese woman, a teacher of religion to small children," concerning the Ramaḍān fast.[30] No direct citations are provided for the key to Kessler's argument, that elections were seen by peasants as an act of collective self-denial and egalitarian self-assertion similar to the pilgrimage and the fast. Just as Talal Asad, in discussing Marxist studies of seventh century Arabia, warns against deducing the "primary motive" of a religious ideology from its major political consequences or reducing "the complex implications of religious texts ... to simple political meanings,"[31] there is the inverse difficulty exemplified by Kessler of inferring, albeit plausibly, the contours of the relation between popular religious ideologies and politics from patterns of achieved political action alone. Moreover, Kessler treats peasant religiosity as relatively fixed. His detailed account of historical changes in landownership, economic conditions and political movements is not matched by an equal (although admittedly more difficult) attempt to suggest what were the major transformations in peasant religiosity, or if there were none, to explain why the Islamically-based peasant conceptions of a general order of existence—to adopt part of Geertz'[32] characterization of religion—were relatively impermeable to the growing impoverishment of peasants. Despite these reservations, Kessler's rather crude characterization of his study as an analytical articulation of "material" and "ideal" factors does not do justice to the much more intricate and rewarding case study which he presents.

"Great" Transformations and Styles of Religiosity

The implications of major changes in political and economic forms and in the intellectual "technology" of how ideas get reproduced and disseminated are just beginning to be explored in the context of Islamic studies and in all probability will have a major impact upon the direction of research over the next few years. Changes in basic patterns of thought and religiosity are often self-evident only in retrospect. Marc Bloch, writing of the "great transformation" of the emergence of feudalism in Europe, wrote that "these generations of men had no conscious desire to create new social forms, nor were they aware of doing so. Instinctively each strove to turn to account the resources provided by the existing social structure and if, unconsciously, something new was eventually created, it was in the process of trying to adapt the old."[33] An example of the sort of "great" transformation under discussion here is Jack Goody's discussion of the impact of literacy upon historically known and contemporary societies and the sociocultural consequences of the introduction of such a new intellectual technology.[34] What concerns us most here is the impact of such major innovations upon religious belief and experience, an important component of how individuals think about their social and spiritual universe and manage to act within it. As Marilyn Waldman has pointed out, Goody relegates his discussion of the implications of the more nuanced problem of restricted versus generalized literacy to the last ten pages of his most recent book, although her own essay concisely suggests how forms of literacy have influenced the formation of early Islamic tradition.[35] In a recent study of Islamic higher education in early twentieth century Morocco, my own point of departure has been the sociology of Pierre Bourdieu. I have sought to depict how the collapse of traditional institutions of learning and the rise to prominence of other educational forms has begun to bring about shifts in what Moroccans consider to be religious knowledge and its appropriate carriers at both the popular level and that of religious specialists.[36]

One of the most important efforts to assess the impact of technological and economic changes upon religious styles and movements is a recent work by Serif Mardin on the Turkish fundamentalist Saïd Nursi (1873-1960), the Bediüzzaman ("Nonpareil of the Times") and founder of the Nur movement.[37] The Nur movement first took shape in western Turkey in the 1920s, and between 1950 and 1975 became international in scope. It developed in the context of Republican Turkey and its leaders gradually learned to work with "modern" ideas and materials. That it became international was in part due to the efforts of a talented translator based in California, and to the fact that the content of its message attracted a "new world clientele" experiencing "the spiritual crisis which accompanied modernization."[38] The movement has no formal organizational structure, thus meeting the challenge of "modernization" in a way almost antithetical to the Egyptian brotherhood studied by Gilsenan. Nor does it have clear boundaries of membership; anyone who joins in its task of disseminating the truth of the Qur'ân is a disciple. In terms of the content of Saïd Nursi's message, Mardin sees him "as using both the Koran and the residues of Anatolian mysticism as a transformational medium which allows him to ... establish contact with popular religion, draw followers of folk Islam in the direction of a belief focused on the unicity of God, shift the dead weight of traditional Islamic orthodoxy and join the stream of an understanding of the laws of nature as they appear in Western European modern thought."[39] Saïd Nursi was aware that he was conveying Islamic doctrine with new emphases, particularly upon the dynamic quality of the Qur'ânic message and its relation to science and the modern world. Mardin is aware of the difficulties of linking explicit ideologies to particular social groups and classes, but indicated that when Saïd Nursi's message was first disseminated in western Turkey (to which he was exiled in the 1920s by the Republican government), it appealed primarily to "the important contingent of small town dwellers with some education but an inconsistent status—part modern, part traditional,'' thus presumably receptive to new forms of religious discourse.[40]

So far this skeletal representation of Mardin's argument suggests that it contains the elements of a fascinating yet theoretically conventional study of an Islamic movement, although even in these terms it is rare that the thinking of a single religious leader is so effectively placed in a socio-historical context. What makes Mardin's study almost unique is his complementary concern with explaining the appeal of Saïd Nursi's message in terms of the ''communications revolution'' that began to be felt in Turkey by the late nineteenth century and of course elsewhere in the world. Patterns of governmental organization and authority changed radically, as well as the forms in which knowledge and information were construed and communicated. Even when persons in authority thought they were using new technologies to preserve the old, new elements and patterns of thought and authority were introduced with the telegraph, newspapers, magazines and an expanded (even if not mass) educational system. Newspapers and magazines, for instance, ''replaced expostulation (with) arguments which were addressed to the presumed shared rationality of the readers.''[41]

This great transformation in modes of communication implicitly affected notions of what was considered to be religious knowledge and discipline as well. Through the nineteenth century, the accepted popular and elite notion of religious knowledge was that it was acquired under the guidance of an acknowledged master, without whom religious insight could not be achieved. This mode of communication also implied new forms of social control introduced with the impact of modernization. In the Nur movement the ''message'' of the founder—his opinions on religious subjects and his commentaries on the Qurʾân (in Turkish, in itself a major innovation)—was more important than his person or personal ties to him. This aspect of the Nur movement is remarkably different from the practices of almost all other Sufi movements. The form of Saïd Nursi's message was thus characterized by ''the written text replacing the instructions of the charismatic leader and the attempt to make the central truths of the Koran intelligible to a wide audience.''[42]

Even if the shift in the technology of intellectual reproduction is not consciously recognized or is even substantially denied, it has had a major impact upon belief and practice throughout the Islamic world. The analysis offered by Mardin offers a necessary link between the microsociological analysis of ideologies, their carriers and their contexts, and the worldwide economic and technological transformations that often have unanticipated implications for religious belief and practice as well as for other aspects of social life.

Conclusion: New Directions

There are several implications to the emerging trends in the study of Islam in local contexts depicted above. When studies of local interpretations of Islam were guided by the assumptions of the great/little tradition dichotomy, religious beliefs and practices frequently were not specifically related to classes or groups within a given society. Nor was much attention given to how such beliefs and practices changed as they pass from one social group or class to another. When adapted to new settings, class or status groups, religious ideologies often have implications far removed from those that were consciously intended by their original carriers. To understand such transformations, concern with the internal differentiation of belief and practice within "local" societies is essential. Moreover, any discussion of class necessitates wider notions of political and economic context than have frequently been utilized in past studies of Islam. Kessler's extensive analysis of regional political and economic transformations is an example of the wider scope required by such studies.

Another good example is Michael Fischer's ethnographic discussion of the interlocking patterns of friendship, discipleship and intermarriage of Shîᶜî *ᶜulamâ᾽* in Qûm and their relation to *madrasa* education and the style of religious discourse conveyed by it. The core of Fischer's discussion of these themes is set against the backdrop of a fairly general account of the historical development of Shîᶜî ideology and religious leadership and the political context in which they have developed. A limited geographical locale is no longer a prerequisite of a study of Islam in a local context; specific categories of religious specialists, as in Fischer's case, can be just as "local." Similarly, Nazîh Ayubi's recent account of the characteristic ideological orientations and backgrounds of participants in Egyptian neofundamentalist movements—he indicates that they are often educated (but significantly not in formal institutions of religious studies, which have a very different clientele), middle class and urban—require as sufficient contextual backdrop Egyptian society as a whole.[43]

What the studies of Kessler, Fischer, Ayubi and others mentioned earlier all have in common is a notion of context wider than earlier anthropological concerns with specific village locales and more narrow than the Islam of all times and places sometimes invoked by scholars and believers with non-sociological views of religious experience. The "middle ground" between these two extremes appears to be the most productive for comprehending world religious traditions. Exploration of this middle ground also facilitates an understanding of how the universalistic elements of Islam are practically communicated and of how modes of communication affect religious "universals." Among crucial topics that have not been sufficiently studied are 1) the pilgrimage to Mecca as a vehicle for disseminating or reformulating popular interpretations of Islam (prior studies have concentrated principally upon the *ḥājj* as a means of confirming social status or as a religious *rite de passage*), 2) the impact of Saudi efforts to fund younger religious teachers from throughout the Islamic world for studies in revitalized (and sect-free) institutions of higher learning in Saudi Arabia, 3) the use of oil revenues to enhance religious movements or institutions in less wealthy Islamic states, and 4) the study of dispersed, transregional "minority" Islamic groups such as the Ismâᶜîlis.

A second major implication of the newer approaches to the study of Islam in local contexts is to reopen in a more constructive way the old debate among Islamic scholars as to what constitutes "normative" beliefs in Islam. In the past, discussion of the notion of normative Islam was often devoid of specific social and political contexts. When in the 1950s the late Gustave E. von Grunebaum considered the various ways in which great and little traditions could relate to one another, one possibility he considered was that the great tradition constituted the norm, the little traditions actual practice.[44] Norms must be carried and at times be imposed by some persons over others; they do not simply exist. The "great transformation" brought about by new forms of communication raise salient questions concerning who accords legitimacy to various "normative" interpretations of Islam. Ayubi makes it clear that Egyptian fundamentalists rarely seek support or approbation from the traditionally educated religious elite or their supporters. Their point of reference is a "new," educated and urbanized audience with rather different religious expectations. The studies by Mardin on Bediüzzaman and by myself on the demise of Islamic mosque-university education in Morocco also suggest the importance of fundamental shifts in the intellectual technology used in transmitting and legitimating religious knowledge and authority. Colonel Qadhdhāfī's *Green Book*, which at least in the English edition advertises that it provides the "ultimate solution" to world problems, nowhere specifically uses the term *Islam* although it can be argued that it is implicitly informed by an appeal to Islamic beliefs and principles.[45] The low esteem of the author of the *Green Book* for the traditional interpreters and arbitors of Islamic tradition could not be more clear.

If current debates over what are "correct" or "normative" interpretations of Islam are particularly intense, they are hardly unique to the present or to the recent past. Now that the first rush of studies on clergy-state relations in Iran has peaked, more historically reflective analyses suggest that there has not been any single "golden age" in which a particular form or doctrinal interpretation of such relations has prevailed, and that the content of what is regarded as normative as well as *whose* norms prevailed in practice has continuously undergone major shifts.[46] What is "traditional" in Islam is necessarily subject to ongoing debate and interpretation, so that the "problem" sometimes raised by scholars in the past of how Islam is accommodated to local and regional realities is somewhat misconstrued. The crucial issue is to elicit the implicit and explicit criteria as to why one interpretation of Islam is considered more normative than others at particular times and places, thus integrally relating ideologies to both their carriers and contexts. So one returns to the necessity of *not* taking meanings for granted. Even in Qurʾānic recitation, which many Muslims regard as the essence of immutable communication, what is communicated is subject necessarily to considerable variation despite the best conscious efforts of reciters. As Richard Martin has written: "In order to know *what* the Koran means we have to ask *how* it means in Muslim culture. To answer this question we need to identify the various contexts—the textual, ritual, social and cosmological spaces—it occupies in Muslim culture."[47] What is recited is central and significant, but inseparable from an account of how the recitation occurs and in what particular context. Without all these elements present, it is difficult to understand what is meant. A recitation of the Qurʾān in seventh century Arabia can take on a very different meaning than its recitation in twentieth-century Afghanistan. Whether the meaning at issue is a Qurʾānic recitation or the wider expressions of religiosity, the renewed study of Islam in local contexts involves greater attention to how religious tradition and religious organization specifically shape and in turn are shaped by the wider political and economic contexts in which they occur.

NOTES

1 Sūra 12, verse 2, *The Meaning of the Glorious Koran*, tr. Mohammed Marmaduke Pickthall (New York: Mentor Books, 1953), p. 174.

2 Abdul Hamid M. el-Zein, *The Sacred Meadows: A Structural Analysis of Religious Symbolism in an East African Town* (Evanston: Northwestern University Press, 1974), p. 172. See also his "Beyond Ideology and Theology: The Search for the Anthropology of Islam," *Annual Review of Anthropology* 6 (1977): 227-54. I owe the phrase "neo-*tauḥīdī*" to John Voll.

3 For example, see Harold B. Barclay, *Buurri al Lamaab: A Suburban Village in the Sudan* (Ithaca: Cornell University Press, 1964), pp. 136-210, who uses "genuine" in this sense, and Fazlur Rahman, *Islam*, 2d ed. (Chicago: University of Chicago Press, 1979), p. 153, who labels the leaders of popular religious orders as "charlatans" and "spiritual delinquents" because of their deviance from his own notion of accepted Islamic tradition. Although the polymath Gustave E. von Grunebaum also tended to juxtapose great and little traditions, the richness of his examples served as a stimulus to critical thought. See, for example, his "The Problem of Unity in Diversity," in Gustave E. von Grunebaum, ed., *Unity and Variety in Muslim Civilization* (Chicago: University of Chicago Press, 1955), pp. 17-37; Richard C. Martin discusses von Grunebaum's Concept of Culture in "Geertz and the Study of Islam: An Evaluation" (paper presented to the American Academy of Religion, San Francisco, Dec. 19-22, 1981).

4 Marshall G. S. Hodgson, *The Venture of Islam*, 3 vols. (Chicago: University of Chicago Press, 1974), vol. 1, p. 80.

5 Edmund Burke, III, "Islamic History as World History: Marshall Hodgson, 'The Venture of Islam,'" *International Journal of Middle East Studies* 10 (1979): 261-62.

6 These are *The Religion of Java* (New York: The Free Press of Glencoe, 1960); *Islam Observed: Religious Development in Morocco and Indonesia* (New Haven: Yale University Press, 1968); and "Suq: The Bazaar Economy in Sefrou," in Clifford Geertz, Hildred Geertz and Lawrence Rosen, *Meaning and Order in Moroccan Society* (New York: Cambridge University Press, 1979), pp. 123-313. For an assessment of the anthropological contribution to the study of Islam in the Middle East, see Dale F. Eickelman, *The Middle East: An Anthropological Approach* (Englewood Cliffs, N.J.: Prentice-Hall, Inc., 1981), pp. 201-260. Significant studies by anthropologists and others dealing with Islam in other regions but not discussed in this essay for reasons of space are I. M. Lewis, ed., *Islam in Tropical Africa*, 2d ed. (Bloomington: Indiana University Press for the International African Institute, 1980); D. B. Cruise O'Brien, *The Mourides of Senegal* (Oxford: Clarendon Press, 1971); John N. Paden, *Religion and Political Culture in Kano* (Berkeley and Los Angeles: University of California Press, 1973); Akbar S. Ahmed, *Millennium and Charisma among Pathans* (Boston: Routledge & Kegan Paul, 1976) (and subsequent works now in preparation); Richard Maxwell Eaton, *Sufis of Bijapur, 1300-1700* (Princeton: Princeton University Press, 1978); W. R. Roff, ed., *Kelan-*

tan: Religion, Society and Politics in a Malay State (Kuala Lumpur: Oxford University Press, 1974). A particularly important recent collection of essays that indicates the state of the art is the special issue of *Annales*, 35, no. 3-4 (May-August 1980), ''Recherches sur l'Islam: Histoire et Anthropologie.''

7 Geertz, *Religion*, p. 7.

8 *Ibid.*, pp. 4, 5-6, 234.

9 *Ibid.*, p. 234.

10 *Ibid.*, p. 379.

11 Geertz, *Islam Observed*, pp. 15, 23-24.

12 Edward W. Said, *Orientalism* (New York: Pantheon Books, 1978), p. 326.

13 Geertz, ''Suq,'' pp. 140-50.

14 *Ibid.*, p. 139.

15 Clifford Geertz, ''Religious Change and Social Order in Soeharto's Indonesia,'' *Asia* (New York) 27 (Autumn 1972): 62-84.

16 *Ibid.*, pp. 70-71.

17 *Ibid.*, pp. 72-73. For an early discussion (originally published 1957) of the problem of change in religious identity and faith, see also Geertz, ''Ritual and Social Change: A Javanese Example,'' in *The Interpretation of Cultures* (New York: Basic Books, Inc., 1973), pp. 142-69. Geertz' approach to ''thick description'' has recently been attacked by Michael M. J. Fischer, *Iran: From Religious Dispute to Revolution* (Cambridge: Harvard University Press, 1980), p. 266, as ''trivial'' because Geertz presumably ''turns away from [an account of] the larger historical and sociological contexts.'' This notion is echoed in Clive S. Kessler, *Islam and Politics in a Malay State: Kelantan 1838-1969* (Ithaca: Cornell University Press, 1978), p. 20, who asserts that Geertz disregards his own warning (in *Interpretation*, p. 30) that cultural analysis should not ''lose touch'' with the political, economic and stratificatory ''hard surfaces of life.'' In my judgment, Geertz recognizes and at times vividly describes these larger contexts and harder surfaces, but has deliberately chosen to clarify problems of cultural meanings, providing only historical and contextual detail appropriate to further their comprehension, than to represent details of political economy reasonably accessible in other works. Hence the question is *how* such larger contexts are invoked in ethnographic and social historical accounts, not whether they are. Thus in Kessler's monograph, discussed in detail later in this essay, his excellent account of the ''harder surfaces'' is complemented by a largely inferential one of popular religious beliefs which takes for granted many of those aspects of systems of meaning that Geertz, despite an occasionally over-luxuriant prose, seeks with some success to elucidate. Perhaps Kessler should be criticized for neglecting what he might call the ''softer'' surfaces of life, surfaces which however are crucial for understanding how persons in a given society perceive their opportunities and alternatives.

18 Michael Gilsenan, *Saint and Sufi in Modern Egypt* (Oxford: Clarendon Press, 1973), pp. 188-207. Another study that uses a Weberian framework (but one divergent from that employed by Gilsenan) is Dale F. Eickelman, *Moroccan Islam: Tradition and Society in a Pilgrimage Center* (Austin: University of Texas Press, 1976). See also my ''Ideological Change and Regional Cults: Maraboutism and Ties of 'Closeness' in Western Morocco,'' in *Regional Cults*, ed. Richard P. Werbner, A.S.A. Monographs, 16 (New York and London: Academic Press, 1977), pp. 3-28.

19 Ali Merad, *Le Réformisme musulmane en Algérie de 1925 à 1940* (Paris and The Hague: Mouton & Co., 1967).

20 Merad, *Réformisme*, pp. 437-439. For another discussion of the implications of Merad's work, see Ernest Gellner, *Muslim Society*, Cambridge Studies in Social Anthropology, 32 (Cambridge and New York: Cambridge University Press, 1981), pp. 149-73. The entire collection of essays in this volume constitute essential reading. In some regions of Algeria the reform movement appears to have been so firmly set in the milieu of maraboutic practices that reformist leaders often came from the same local maraboutic families that dominated other forms of religious expression and practice. See Fanny Colonna, ''L'Islaḥ

en milieu paysan: le cas de l'Aurès 1936-1938,'' *Revue algérienne des sciences juridiques, économiques et politiques* 14 (1977): 277-88.

21 See Dale F. Eickelman, ''The Art of Memory: Islamic Education and Its Social Reproduction,'' *Comparative Studies in Society and History* 20 (1978): 485-516, and *Moroccan Islam*, pp. 211-37, for an account of historical shifts in popular religious assumptions; also Rafiuddin Ahmed, ''Islamization in Nineteenth Century Bengal,'' Krishna Gopal, ed., *Contributions to South Asian Studies, 1* (Delhi: Oxford University Press, 1979), pp. 88-119.

22 Kessler, *Islam and Politics*, p. 20.

23 *Ibid.*, pp. 32-33, 35.

24 Max Weber, *The Sociology of Religion*, tr. Ephraim Fishcoff (Boston: Beacon Press, 1963), p. 263.

25 Kessler, *Islam and Politics*, pp. 210-13.

26 *Ibid.*, p. 208.

27 *Ibid.*, pp. 232-34.

28 Particularly the studies of William R. Roff, including *The Origins of Malay Nationalism* (New Haven: Yale University Press, 1967), and the various contributors to Roff, ed., *Kelantan.*

29 James Siegel, *The Rope of God* (Berkeley and Los Angeles: University of California Press, 1969).

30 Kessler, *Islam and Politics*, pp. 218-19.

31 Talal Asad, ''Ideology, Class and the Origin of the Islamic State,'' *Economy and Society* 9 (1980): 460.

32 Geertz, *Interpretation*, p. 90.

33 Marc Bloch, *Feudal Society*, tr. L. A. Manyon (Chicago: University of Chicago Press, 1964), p. 148,

34 Jack Goody, *The Domestication of the Savage Mind* (Cambridge and New York: Cambridge University Press, 1977).

35 Marilyn R. Waldman, ''Primitive Mind/Modern Mind: New Approaches to an Old Problem Applied to Religion,'' in Richard C. Martin, ed., *Islam and the History of Religions: Perspectives on the Study of a Religious Tradition* (Berkeley: Berkeley Series in Religious Studies, in press).

36 Eickelman, ''Art of Memory,'' esp. pp. 510-12.

37 Serif Mardin, ''Bediüzzaman Saïd Nursi: Preliminary Approaches to the Biography of a Turkish Muslim Fundamentalist Thinker.'' Manuscript, 1981. Cited by permission.

38 Mardin, ''Bediüzzaman,'' I, pp. 3-4.

39 *Ibid.*, IV, p. 9.

40 *Ibid.*, I, p. 31.

41 *Ibid.*, I, p. 13.

42 *Ibid.*, I, p. 19.

43 Fischer, *Iran*, pp. 61-135; Nazîh N. M. Ayubi, ''The Political Revival of Islam: The Case of Egypt,'' *International Journal of Middle East Studies* 12 (1980): 481-99. On Egypt, see also the factually interesting but analytically thin study by Saad Eddin Ibrahim, ''Anatomy of Egypt's Militant Islamic Groups: Methodological Note and Preliminary Findings,'' *International Journal of Middle East Studies* 12 (1980): 423-53; on Iran a useful complement to Fischer is Shahrough Akhavi, *Religion and Politics in Contemporary Iran* (Albany: State University of New York Press, 1980).

44 Von Grunebaum, ''Unity and Variety,'' p. 30.

45 Muammar al-Qathafi, *The Green Book* (Tripoli: Public Establishment for Publishing, Advertising and Distribution, n.d.). In the Arabic version the term *dîn* (religion) is used throughout the text.

46 See Saïd Amir Arjomand, ''Religion, Political Action and Legitimate Domination in Shiᶜite Iran: Fourteenth to Eighteenth Centuries A.D.,'' *Archives Européenes de Sociologie* 20 (1979): 59-109, and his ''The Shiᶜite Hierocracy and the State in Pre-Modern Iran: 1785-1890,'' *Archives Européenes de Sociologie* 22 (1981): 40-78; Nikki R. Keddie, ''Iran: Change in Islam; Islam and Change,'' *International Journal of Middle East Studies* 11 (1980):

531; and William M. Floor, "The Revolutionary Character of the Iranian Ulama: Wishful Thinking or Reality," *International Journal of Middle East Studies* 12 (1980): 501-524.

47 Richard C. Martin, "Understanding the Koran in Text and Context," unpublished manuscript in the author's possession, 1980, p. 28; also his "Structural Analysis and the Qur'an: Newer Approaches to the Study of Islamic Texts," *Journal of the American Academy of Religion* 47 (1980): 665-83.

Contributions to Asian Studies, Vol. XVII

Reflections on Popular Muslim Poetry

ANNEMARIE SCHIMMEL
Harvard University, Cambridge, Massachusetts, U.S.A.

SOME YEARS AGO, a Western-educated Pakistani critic blamed the writers of *marsiyas*—that famous genre of Urdu poetry in which the sufferings of Imam Husain and his family before and during the battle of Karbala are poetically described at great length—for transposing the setting of their tales from seventh-century Arabia to nineteenth-century India and thus being not faithful to historical facts.[1]

The *marsiya* writers were, to my feeling, however, perfectly justified in their approach, for it has been a tradition not only in Islam but in all major religious traditions to interpret the main events of sacred history on a local level so as to give the people the feeling of actual participation in them and not merely as spectators who gaze at an exotic, fascinating or awe-inspiring event far removed in time and space. In fact, this interaction between the scriptural text or sacred historical events and the later generations in various geographical settings is a most important aspect of the history of religion, as Wilfred Cantwell Smith has shown more than once.[2]

Such assimilation of traditions to the local scene is perhaps strongest in the Indian environment. India's assimilative power has often been recognized by foreign observers, and while Turkish and Persian religious poetry generally remain more or less faithful to the classical, Arabic tradition, at least one trend in Indian Islam tends to transform the events of the life of the Prophet and his descendants into "inner Indian" events. India was connected in a special way with the Prophet Muhammad. As legend has it, the south Indian king, Shakarwatī Farmāḍ, had witnessed the splitting of the moon and thus became the first Indian Muslim.[3] And was not India the true home of prophethood, since Adam had stayed in Sarandīb (Ceylon) after being expelled from Paradise?[4]

In the late sixteenth century, a Gujarati poet who described the miraculous events at the Prophet's birth, introduced a brāhman who was present at the auspicious moment and presented the newborn child with the brāhmanical thread.[5] Medieval poetry in Bengal went even farther. In an epic dealing with the Prophet, a fifteenth-century Bengali poet tells the whole story of Creation and describes Brahmā, Vishnu, and Śiva as kinds of prophets, forerunners of the Prophet of Islam, just as in central Islamic traditions Adam, Abraham, Moses, and other Qur'ānic prophets would have been introduced.[6] Apparently the Bengali author felt by no means uncomfortable when inventing such an equation of Muslim/Hindu cosmologies, and it is not known whether any of the orthodox scholars attacked this approach in an area where, as we know, syncretism was widespread and where "the holy brahmin would recite Maulana Rumi's *Mathnawi*" as early as the late fifteenth century.[7] For this reason the area became a special target of movements of reformation and purification in the nineteenth century.

As the Bengali poet showed Muhammad to be the last link in the chain of prophets, who abrogated the previous religious systems, the Ismāʿīlīs, particularly the Satpanthīs, reached even more astonishing forms of prophetology: in some of their *ginān*s, the Ismāʿīlī religious poems—which in part go back to the Middle Ages, and especially in the genre known as *Daśa Avatāra*—Muhammad and ʿAlī are depicted in line with Hindu deities. While Muhammad is usually equated with Brahmā, and Fāṭima with Sarasvatī, ʿAlī assumes the highest rank, namely that of Vishnu's long awaited tenth *avatāra*, who will finally complete the salvation of the world, and religious pictures may show him, blueish like Krishna, even with four arms, his white mule Duldul being attended by Hanumān.[8] Another aspect of Indianization is the use of Indian names for God, who may be called *Gosain*, *Īśvara*, *Kartār* instead of Allah. This seems to have been common in Bengali, but is known also from Sind and the Punjab. The wide incidence of this practice is evidenced by the fact that the *sharīʿat*-bound Suhrawardī saint of Ucch, Makhdūm-i Jahāniyān Jahāngasht (d. 1385), prohibited the use of Indian names of God in popular worship.

These few random examples show that the message of Islam could become more or less permeated by indigenous elements, just as in some parts of India a remarkable blending of architectural elements took place so that, for instance, in Ahmadabad some of the mosques "assume the inwardness of an Indian temple," as M. Mujeeb has correctly remarked.[9] It would be worthwhile to find out what influence Ismāʿīlī preachers, who came to Gujarat from the twelfth century onward and who were responsible for the Islamization of part of the population, may have had on such syncretism in architecture. The situation is, in a certain way, comparable to the teachings of the Ismāʿīlī leaders, who often appeared in the garb of Sufi masters and like them taught a spiritualized form of Islam; hence, many Ismāʿīlī *ginān*s are almost indistinguishable from mystical folk poetry in Sindhi and Gujarati.

It goes without saying that this syncretistic trend was never liked by the orthodox Muslims in the Subcontinent, and it is not difficult to discern two constantly interacting strands of Islamic attitudes in India, which we may call "mystico-syncretistic" and "prophetic-separatistic." Richard Eaton's distinction between "adhesion" and "reform" points to the same dichotomy. The former tended to assimilate Indian traditions and is largely found on the nonurban level, even though some leading Sufi masters, especially in the Chishti tradition, and some ruling princes participated in this trend or encouraged it: not only should Akbar and Dārā Shikōh be mentioned in this regard but also "Bādshāh" Zainul-ʿĀbidīn of Kashmir (reg. 1420-1470) and Akbar's contemporaries in the Deccan, Muhammad-Qulī Quṭbshāh of

Golconda (reg. 1580-1612) and Ibrāhīm II ʿAdilshāh of Bijapur (reg. 1580-1626). While in their realms an harmonious blending of at least some elements of both cultures (particularly fine arts and music) took place, the "orthodox" Muslims never really felt at home in India. They were largely the descendants of Arabic, Turkish, or Persian immigrants who were, and still are, well aware of their roots outside India.[10] They would probably have agreed with Shāh Walīʾullāh who, in the eighteenth century, voiced the opinion that, "We are Arabs, whose fathers have fallen in exile in India."[11]

It was this strong and influential group of "Mecca-oriented" Muslims whose roots lay outside the Subcontinent (as already the historian Baranī had stressed in the mid-fourteenth century) who preserved the divine law as carefully as possible. They relentlessly fought against the innovations that grew on Indian soil, particularly against the veneration of saints in which they—to a certain extent correctly—saw the continuation of pre-Islamic customs.[12] Indeed, quite a few sanctuaries of Sufi saints are built on the sites of former temples, and legend often tells that this or that saint deliberately chose, or appropriated by miracle, a former Hindu site of worship or place of pilgrimage for his residence. One of the most famous examples is the shrine of Laʿl Shahbāz Qalandar in Sehwan on the lower Indus, the old Śivistan, "place of Śiva." Some of the illicit practices connected with this place, which is charged with awe-inspiring power, have always been condemned by the orthodox as is the case with the shrine in Nurpur/Islamabad, built on the site of an old Zoroastrian fire temple which was then used as a Buddhist place of worship, or with the shrine of Sālār Masʿūd in Bahraich, Uttar Pradesh, allegedly erected on the site of a sun temple.[13] Sacred animals found near a number of shrines (crocodiles at Mangho Pir/Karachi, white softshell turtles at Bāyazīd Bisṭāmī's [!] shrine in Chittagong, peacocks in Kallakahar/Salt Range, fishes in Sylhet, to mention only some well-known examples) add to the "Indian-ness" of many of these frequently visited shrines. We cannot blame the orthodox who, in trying to maintain the purity of the religion of the "Arabic Prophet," were horrified by these popular developments; reformers appeared time and again to call people back to an unpolluted Islam. Even inside the "mystical" tradition this tension can be witnessed in the numerous medieval tales about the *qalandar*s, generally connected with a lower, indigenous stratum. They would annoy the well-established Sufi saints, who invariably belonged to the *ashrāf* and often were *sayyid*s, and as such many of the saints were also in the forefront of preserving the Prophetic tradition.

Yet, the "mystical" tradition developed into something that appealed to the masses. Islamic mysticism had begun as an elitist form of religion—the religion of the few who tried to comply to the prescriptions of the Qurʾān even more seriously and with deeper emotional strength than did the masses. These early Indian Sufis tried to realize the central duty of a Muslim, the uncompromising *tauḥīd* [attesting God's Unity], in their whole lives. Sufism then became a kind of mass movement thanks to the activities of the orders which appeared on the scene in the mid-twelfth century. They brought the high ideals of love of God and His Prophet and of the attainment of spiritual salvation by means of emotion, rather than bookish erudition, to large groups of the faithful who longed for a more personal relation with the Divine than the traditional forms of Islams could give them at this point. Even though the Sufis in the course of time became very productive authors of books in which they displayed an extraordinary skill in developing complicated, sometimes even abstruse, metaphysical systems, yet, the true ideal of mystical Islam was immediate knowledge from God, *ᶜilm ladunnī* (Sūra 18:65), and the model of the "unlettered Prophet," *al-nabī al-ummī* (Sūra 7:157) was always before them: they too hoped to be filled with divine wisdom without the mediation of learned works. Hence many folk poets in Turkey called themselves *ummi* (Ummi Sinan, Ummi Kemal, etc.). The legend that this or that leading Sufi poet was illiterate and could read only the letter *alif*, the cypher for God's unity and unicity, looms large in hagiographical works from Turkey to the Subcontinent, even though these very poets display a great variety of scholarly achievements which they cleverly introduce into their poetry.

The anti-intellectual bias of this mystical tradition appealed, understandably, to the illiterate population of Anatolia, Afghanistan, of the Indian plains; they loved the poets who told them in their mother tongue—be it Sindhi or Panjabi, Pashto or Bengali—that *kanz qudūrī kāfiya* are of no avail for the loving seeker of God: neither the handbook of tradition compiled by ᶜAlī al-Muttaqī of Burhanpur (d. 1565 in Mecca), nor the compendium of Ḥanafī jurisprudence by Qudūrī (d. 1037), which was taught in the madrasas from the very beginning of Islamic education in India, nor the rules of Arabic grammar are important for him who contemplates the Face of the Beloved.

Lōkān ṣarf u naḥw - mūñ muṭāliᶜu supriñ

[Leave] the people with grammar and syntax, I contemplate the Beloved,

sings Qāḍī Qādan in Sind (d. 1551) and expresses the central feeling of the mystical folk poets.[14] These poets, be they in Anatolia or in India, reverted therefore to their native languages, a process which dates back to the late thirteenth century in Turkey, and somewhat later in India, where it reached its zenith in the eighteenth century.[15]

The role of the Sufis in the development of the regional languages can be compared to that of the European mystics (Mechtild von Magdeburg, Julian of Norwich, Jacopone da Todi and others) for the development of the modern European literary languages. The Muslim poets adopted the native poetical forms: instead of using the complicated Arabo-Persian quantitative meters they reverted in Turkey to syllable-counting meters which they mostly used in four-lined stanzas with a rhyme common to the fourth lines, while in India forms like the *dōha* were used and strung together in longer poems, and singable forms like the *kāfī* soon emerged. A form barely found in high literature, the *sīḥarfī* or Golden Alphabet, is common in folk poetry all over the Islamic countries, even in Swahili, for it is an excellent help in memorizing both the alphabet and the major religious events, duties or concepts. In India, the *bārahmāsā*, "poems about the twelve months," were utilized by Muslim mystical folk poets to express the longing of the soul for the heavenly beloved during the seasons of the year, either in the Indian sequence of months, or in the Muslim lunar calendar (lately in Sindhi even the Christian months have been used for *bārahmāsā*).[16] In order to appeal to the masses, and particularly to the women, the poets reverted to images taken from daily life so that weaving and spinning, grinding corn and churning butter are elevated to symbols of spiritual activities (a trend also visible in Rumi's verse!), and the women could sing these simple verses while performing their household duties, learning through them the basic facts of Islamic lore.[17]

In the Indian tradition, this latter aspect of mystical folk poetry is particularly important, for the traditional Hindu ideal of the *virahiṇī*, the woman longing for her beloved or husband, was adopted into the Islamic setting, and the soul, (*nafs*, always described and blamed as a "nasty female" by the early ascetics of Arabia and Iran) appears now as the "woman soul" that braves all difficulties on the path towards her beloved until she slowly reaches the lofty stage of *nafs muṭmaʾinna*, "the soul at peace" (Sūra 89:27) on which she is called to return to her Lord, united with Him by death. The tragic folk tales of the Indus valley in which the heroine usually dies in her attempt to find the beloved formed an excellent basis for these ideas: the Sufi *ṭarīqa* was poetically described in terms taken from Sassui's wandering through the desert, or Sohni's crossing the Indus to meet her friend.[18]

One should not overlook the fact that the longed-for beloved is at times not God but rather the Prophet. In the *bārahmāsā* the maiden soul may express her intense longing to reach the last resting place of the Prophet in Medina in the last month of the year after visiting Mecca for the *ḥajj*: Muhammad becomes the "bridegroom of Madina," and the clouds that will bring rain (*raḥma*, "mercy", as the Prophet was sent *raḥmatan lilᶜālamīn*, Sūra 21:107) reminds the Sindhi poet of the black curls of the beloved Prophet, the red lightning of his red, festive attire.[19] In the Ismāᶜīlī *ginān*s, again, it is the Imam who is the longed-for spiritual beloved.[20]

The important role of the Prophet as the highest goal on the mystical Path has often been overlooked by critics of popular Sufi poetry. To be sure, many ballads describe Muhammad and his miracles in glowing colors, and one reads with delight the various accounts of the stories of the sighing palm trunk or the speaking gazelle, repeated over the centuries. Even though these ballads usually rely on well-known traditions, some of them seem to have been common to Turkey and India while they are, as far as I can see, unknown in the Arabic world. Among them is the story of the bees which hum the *ṣalawāt ᶜalā Muḥammad* [prayerful blessing upon the Prophet] while entering the beehive, and it is thanks to this formula of blessing that their honey becomes sweet![21] Muhammad's miracles are described at length, and the poems about his heavenly journey abound in wonderful, simple images. Yunus Emre describes in unassuming verses how God orders Gabriel to take out Burāq so that the Prophet may mount it, admire His throne, look at the angels in their green garments, and smell the roses of Paradise. Such poems, which belonged to the favorite repertoire of popular Sufi poets, are reminiscent of the prints of Burāq with lovely painted face and curly hair as they are sold in the courtyards of Indian shrines; or of the superbly attired Burāqs painted on the backs of trucks and tank wagons in Pakistan and Afghanistan.[22] The popular veneration of and love for the Prophet (who is symbolized on such pictures by a little cloud or a white rose) find an outlet in these kinds of ''primitive'' descriptions which, however, could infuse delight into a child's soul and fill it with loving admiration for the wonderful Prophet, who performed so many miracles and who will finally intercede for his community on the Last Day.

Muhammad was even more than a leader and intercessor, guide and representative of God's mercy: he had been transformed in medieval theosophy into a metaphysical power, and in time it became the goal of Sufis to attain not the ever in-accessible Essence of God but rather the *ḥaqīqa muḥammadiyya*, the ''archetypal Muhammad,'' the meeting point of the created human world with the sphere of the Divine. The journey toward this goal, which leads the mystic through the different spheres of the pre-Muhammadan prophets, was often described by Sufis, particularly by the founders of some of the orders such as the Badawiyya and Dasūqiyya in Egypt, in whose verses (written in a rather unclassical Arabic) the recurrent theme seems to be:

> I was with Noah during the flood,
> I was with Jesus, I was with Moses on Mount Sinai, (etc.).[23]

What this means is that the poet claims to have reached union with the *ḥaqīqa muḥammadiyya* which includes all the stages of the previous prophets. This was the kind of poetry that was generally adopted in mystical circles. Through the centuries almost every poet or poetaster between Morocco and Bengal would tend to repeat these and similar statements to point to his own lofty rank so that this branch of popular poetry tends to become rather monotonous.

Furthermore, popular poetry as it generally developed with the expansion of the mystical orders from the second half of the thirteenth century onward, is deeply indepted to Ibn al-ᶜArabī, not only for his elaboration of the theory of the Perfect Man and the *ḥaqīqa muḥammadiyya*, but even more for the system of *waḥdat al-wujūd* which he had ingeniously built up, summing up and reinterpreting the expressions and experiences of previous generations of Sufis. *Waḥdat al-wujūd* ''unity of Being'' became after 1300 indeed a kind of umbrella concept for most mystical orders, and even those who disagreed with its theoretical foundations could not help using Ibn al-ᶜArabī's terminology. It therefore percolated down to the masses who listened to mystical leaders who spoke about the all-embracing and all-pervading Unity in which every problem seemed to be solved very easily. ''Everything is He,'' as the short formula claimed; it is a formula which is one of the basic ingredients of mystical verse after A.D. 1300, it accounts for the similarity of expression wherever members of the fraternities sung of their religious experience.

India was a particularly fertile soil for Islamic mystical notions of divine unicity. Similarities between the theories of *waḥdat al-wujūd* and Indian *advaita* philosophy have always been underlined by Hindus, but also by Western students of Sufism, even though it is not correct to equate the two systems.[24] One can however not blame those critics who saw nothing but "measureless pantheism" in verses like those of the Panjabi Sufi Bullhē Shāh (d. 1752 in Qasur) who claimed that there is no real difference between Moses and Pharaoh, or between Abū Ḥanīfa and Hanumān, for "everything is He." Bullhē Shāh also claimed with innumerable other mystical poets that he was neither Hindu nor Turk nor Peshawari.[25] The first example reminds us of the adoption of Hanumān into the *Daśa Avatāra* stories of the Ismāᶜīlī tradition in which the resourceful monkey also became a faithful servant of ᶜAlī, while the second one recalls the old dichotomy of Turk and Hindu, used as a symbol in classical Persian poetry but assuming a very factual meaning in Indian Islam: the Turk is equated with the powerful Muslim rulers and the Hindu, with the lowly blackish slave.[26] In Baranī's statement that the true Muslim ruler has to be a Turk, and that even the Muslims of Indian origin are not fully accepted into the hierarchy, these ideas were clearly put before the reader. In the light of essential unity, however, none of these distinctions has any meaning for the ecstatic mystical poet.

When one reads this largely syncretistic folk poetry, which developed mainly in the plains of the Indus and the Five Rivers as in Bengal (but less frequently among the Pathans who retained, as it were, the more sober tradition of the Khorasani and Ghaznavid Sufis) one is not too surprised that the Mecca-oriented intelligentsia of the Subcontinent thouroughly disliked such verse. Urban mystics might note down their experiences on the path toward the *ḥaqīqa muḥammadiyya* or their firm belief in Ibn al-ᶜArabī's system in beautifully phrased Arabic or Persian treatises, as did Khwāja Mir Dard (d. 1785 in Delhi),[27] but then these thoughts would be available only to a few elect disciples. Shāh Walīʾullāh may have had in mind the unbridled utterances of popular Sufis and their far-reaching claims to "mystical union" which made them stand beyond good and evil, when he made the remark that "the books of the Sufis may be an elixir for the elite but are deadly poison for the masses."[28] His criticism was taken up in our century by Muhammad Iqbal who condemned the "mystical" approach to Islam, intending, however, with this verdict only the school of Ibn al-ᶜArabī and its echoes in poetry. To Muhammad Iqbal, the constant repetition of the same topic of all-pervading unity seemed dangerous for the free, dynamic development of the human personality and for man's fruitful dialogue with a personal God as He had revealed Himself in the Qurʾān and as He was experienced by the early Sufis for whom the highest goal was not so much "the lifting of the veils of ignorance" but uniformity of man's will with the Divine Will.

The foreign observer will detect much beauty and tenderness in the popular poetry of Turkey and Indo-Pakistan: one finds delightful descriptions of nature, far away from the standardized topoi of high poetry. One also finds a true concern for the poor. Poetical images are inspired not by precious gardens studded with jewel-like flowers but by the life of lonely shepherds or women who spend the rainy nights without cover, of grainhorders and fishermen, who struggle through the treacherous waves, guided only by the unfailing helmsman, the Prophet. And the landscape—be it the austere hills of Eastern Anatolia or the rivers in the Subcontinent—becomes alive and meaningful in the best of these mystical folk poems. They doubtlessly add a new, fresh color to the hybrid Persian high culture and later to the even more refined and sophisticated Ottoman Turkish and Urdu literatures and are therefore likely to appeal to a Western reader more than the often highly cerebral religious poetry of elite poets from Istanbul or Delhi. The poets of these songs—whether their names are known or have fallen into oblivion—certainly succeeded in creating an overall Islamic world view among the population. Only in rare cases, however, was their deep conviction to become a true, faithful Muslim, a lover of God and His Prophet, expressed in their verse in terms of separatism, or by drawing sharp lines between the two major communities of the Subcontinent. Hindus used to become members of some Sufi orders, predominantly the Chishti, and participated in singing the praise of the Prophet and the saints, and the centers of Islamic mystical piety such as Ajmer or Nizamuddin in Delhi, are still being visited by members of all communities. One should also not forget the role of religious music which was practised in the Chishti and some other *dargāh*s: here again Indian and Islamic elements were successfully blended. Music, however, has always been watched with deep mistrust by the orthodox *ᶜulamāᵓ*, who sensed that its emotional power was able to break down the barriers between individuals and groups and to transgress the boundaries of what was permitted by the religious law.

For these reasons, the manifestations of popular piety have always been watched with apprehension by a considerable number of Indian Muslims. Attempts at purging the rites at certain Sufi shrines or the preaching of "traditional," orthodox Islam to those who seemed to be only superficially Islamized are a constant feature of Indian Islam from the Middle Ages. For the orthodox Muslims always wanted to remind their coreligionists that the true center of their religion was Arabia, and that the Arabian Prophet ("Muḥammad-i makkī-i madīnī, the Hāshimite, Quraishite and Muṭṭālibī" as Qudsi calls him in a commonly used phrase) is the only reliable guide in this world and the next.[29]

We can explain this situation in terms such as the *ashrāf-ajlāf* dichotomy, or as "adhesion and reform." Or we can see, for instance, Dārā Shikōh and Aurangzēb as personifications of these two tendencies at the level of politics. But we can observe them equally clearly in religious poetry. In contrast to the Sindhi folktale of Sohni, elaborated most beautifully in its mystical meaning by Shāh ᶜAbdul Laṭīf Bhitāᵓī (d. 1752), stands Iqbal's "prophetical" song. On the way toward her beloved, Sohni drowns in the Indus (the old Indian motif of being transformed by submersion in water comes in): she gives herself as it were to the all-embracing "mystical" tradition of the Subcontinent, while

Iqbal himself claims to be *Zindarūd*, the "Living Stream" of the prophetic tradition. Or, even more clearly, he assumes the role of the "voice of the caravan bell" in the caravan led by the Prophet, which will finally reach Mecca, the only place where unpolluted Islam is found and the dangerous generalisations of mystical folk poetry are no longer heard.[30]

NOTES

1 Annemarie Schimmel, *Islam in the Indian Subcontinent* (Leiden: E.J. Brill, 1980), p. 177.

2 Wilfred Cantwell Smith, "The True Meaning of Scripture: An Empirical Historian's Non-reductionist Interpretation of the Qurʾān," *International Journal of Middle Eastern Studies* 2 (1980): 487-505.

3 Yohanan Friedmann, "Qiṣṣat Shakarwatī Farmāḍ," *Israel Oriental Studies* 5 (1975): 233-58.

4 This is a theme used in Indo-Muslim literature from Amīr Khusrau (d. 1325) to the polyhistor Ghulām ʿAlī Azād Bilgrāmī (d. 1785) in his *Subḥat al-marjān.*

5 M. J. Dar, "Gujarat's Contribution to Gujari and Urdu," *Islamic Culture* 27 (1953): 33.

6 Richard M. Eaton, "Approaches to the Study of Conversion in Muslim India," in *Islam and the History of Religions*, ed. Richard C. Martin (Berkeley: Berkeley Religious Studies Series [forthcoming]), p. 12 of author's MS, quoting from Asim Roy, "Islam in the Environment of Medieval Bengal," (Ph.D. thesis, Australian National University, 1970), p. 189 ff. See also Qadi Abdal Mannan, "Sufi Literature in Bengal," in *Literary Heritage of Bengal*, mimeographed (New York n.d. [ca. 1974]), pp. 10-11.

7 See Schimmel, *Indian Subcontinent* pp. 49-50 for further examples of Bengali syncretism.

8 Gulshan Khakee, "The Dasa Avatara of the Satpanthi Ismailis and the Imam Shahis of Indo-Pakistan" (Ph.D. thesis, Harvard University, 1972). For the whole development see Azim Nanji, *The Nizārī Ismāʿīlī Tradition in the Indo-Pakistan Subcontinent*, (New York: Caravan Books, 1978).

9 Mohammad Mujeeb, *Islamic Influence on Indian Society* (Meerut: Meenakshi Prakashan, 1972), p. 5.

10 Cf. also Imtiaz Ahmad, "The *ashrāf-ajlāf* dichotomy in Muslim social structure in India," *Indian Economic and Social History Review* 3 (1966).

11 Shah Walīʾullāh, *al-Tafhīmat al-ilāhiyya*, ed. Ghulām Muṣṭafā Qāsimī (Hyderabad/Sind 1966), vol. 2, p. 246.

12 For the whole problem see Sir Thomas Arnold, "Saints, Muhammadan, India" in *Encyclopedia of Religion and Ethics*, ed. James Hastings, vol. 11, pp. 68-73.

13 Kerrin Gräfin Schwerin, "Heiligenverehrung im indischen Islam: Die Legende des Märtyrers Sālār Masʿūd Ghāzī," *Zeitschrift der Deutschen Morgenländischen Gesellschaft* 126/2 (1976).

14 *Qāḍi Qādan jō kalām*, ed. Hiran Thakur (Delhi 1978), Appendix Nr. 2, and Nr. 1.

15 Maulwi ʿAbdul Ḥaqq, *Urdū kī nashw u numā meñ ṣūfiyā-i kirām kā kām* (Karachi, 1954) deals with the impact of the mystics on the early development of Urdu; Annemarie Schimmel, *As through a veil, Mystical Poetry in Islam*, (New York: Columbia University Press, 1982), Chapter 4.

16 Charlotte Vaudeville, *Bārahmāsā, les chansons des douze mois dans les littératures indo-aryennes*, (Pondichéry, 1965).

17 Richard M. Eaton, *Sufis of Bijapur* (Princeton, N.J.: Princeton University Press, 1978), pp. 160-65. In his article cited in note 6 above on "Conversion," p. 16, he maintains that the Sufis "were little inclined to look to the unlettered folk of rural India as potential disciples." That may be true for some very sophisticated masters, but the interest of the "lower classes" in the presence of the mystical guides is quite well established in literature.

18 See Herbert T. Sorley, *Shah Abdul Latif of Bhit* (Oxford: Oxford University Press, 1940 [repr. 1965]); Motilal Jotwani, *Shah Abdul Latif, Life and Works* (Delhi, 1975); Annemarie Schimmel, *Pain and Grace*, Part II (Leiden: E. J. Brill, 1977).

19 Shāh ᶜAbdul Laṭīf, *Shāh jō Risālō*, ed. Kalyan Adwani (Bombay, 1958).

20 Cf. Ali Asani, "The Ismaili *ginān* Literature, Its Structure and Love Symbolism," (Honors thesis, Harvard Univ., 1977).

21 For these and related examples see Annemarie Schimmel, *Und Muhammad ist Sein Prophet* (Cologne: Diederichs, 1981), pp. 76 ff.

22 Schimmel, *Und Muhammad*, pp. 154 ff.

23 Cf. ᶜAli Ṣafī Ḥusain, *Al-adab aṣ-ṣūfī fī Miṣr fi'l-qarn as-sābiᶜ lil-ḥijra* (Cairo 1964).

24 See the approach of Lajwanti Ramakrishna, *Panjabi Sufi Poets* (London-Calcutta, 1938 [repr. Delhi, 1975]) and the review article by Johann Fück, "Die sufische Dichtung in der Landessprache des Panjab," *Orientalistische Literaturzeitung* 42 (1940).

25 Bullhē Shāh, *Dīwān*, ed. Faqir M. Faqir (Lahore 1960), contains numerous examples of this style; in Sindhi the most outstanding representative of this current is Sachal Sarmast (d. 1826); see his *Risālō Sindhī*, ed. Othman Ali Ansari (Karachi 1958), and his *Siraikī Kalām*, ed. M. Ṣādiq Rānīpūrī (Karachi, 1959).

26 Annemarie Schimmel, "Turk and Hindu, a Poetical Image and Its Application to Historical Fact," in Speros Vryonis, Jr., ed. *Islam and Cultural Change in the Middle Ages*, 4th Levi della Vida Conference (Wiesbaden: Otto Harrassowitz, 1975).

27 Schimmel, *Pain and Grace*, Part I.

28 Shāh Walīʾullāh, *Alṭāf al-quds*, p. 95, quoted in M. Jalbānī, *Shāh Walīullāh jō taᶜlīm* (Hyderabad/Sind, 1961), p. 114.

29 This is the beginning of Qudsi Mashhadi's (d. 1654) famous and oft-quoted *naᶜt*. The epithet "Arab" is much more frequently used for the Prophet in Indian literature than elsewhere.

30 Muhammad Iqbāl, *Bāng-i Darā*, final verse of the *Tarāna-i millī*. The soubriquet *Zindarūd* is adopted by him in the *Jāvīdnāma* and has a connection with the image of the Prophet as a "living stream"; cf. Iqbal's Persian rendering of Goethe's "Mahomets Gesang" as *Jū-yi ab* in *Payām-i Mashriq*.

Contributions to Asian Studies, Vol. XVII

Islam in India

The Function of Institutional Sufism in the Islamization of Rajasthan, Gujarat and Kashmir

BRUCE B. LAWRENCE
Duke University, Durham, North Carolina, U.S.A.

THERE IS GENERAL CONSENSUS among scholars of Islamic India that Sufism contributed to the characteristic tone as well as the geographical extent of Islam in the subcontinent of Asia. Less attention has been given, however, to what kind of Sufi activity flourished in Muslim communities south of the Hindu Kush mountain range, especially during the early centuries (roughly 1200-1500) prior to the rise of the Indo-Timuri or Mughal military patronage state. Our intent is to examine the early development of Sufism in Rajasthan, Gujarat and Kashmir, but before discussing developments labeled "Sufi" in any single region, we must first be clear about the profile of Sufism which had gradually evolved outside South Asia in the non-Indian Islamic world. By 1200 Sufism had passed through its classical to its medieval phase. It was no longer the theoretical musings of ascetical protest groups; it had become an institutional movement, with hierarchial orders (*silsila*s; *ṭarīqa*s), charismatic leaders (*pīr*s, *murshid*s, *shaykh*s) and delineated territories of spiritual jurisdiction (*vilāyats*). It also included property: residential buildings or hospices (*khānaqā*s), often related to tomb complexes (*mazār*s), mosques (*masjid*s) and schools (*madrasa*s).

Profiles of Sufism: A Reassessment

It is necessary to recognize the difference between the two phases of Sufism. It is also essential, however, not to prejudge the relative worth of each. The tendency of most Western scholarship, with few exceptions, has been to glorify the first phase and debunk the second. G. Anawati, for instance, writing in *The Legacy of Islam*, states that there were three great periods in Islamic mysticism: the first, from the seventh to the ninth centuries, was characterized in his view as "the struggle for existence"; the second, from the ninth to the twelfth centuries, he saw as an attempt at reconciliation and doctrinal triumph through Imām Ghazzālī (d. 1111), while the third, from the twelfth to the fifteenth centuries, ushered in the mystical orders. A fourth period, from the sixteenth century on, is summarily dismissed as "decadence."[1] Anawati, like H. A. R. Gibb before him, tended to assume that Ghazzālī was the touchstone for all that followed him, despite the fact that his teaching became more and more neutralized as the orders became more and more localized, i.e., "coloured by folklore and by the survival of ancestral customs."[2] Even those scholars who write with zest about the quality of life in the regional Sufi fraternities have tended to accept the judgment that nothing of intellectual, theological or mystical insight was generated through their structures. Hence K. A. Nizami, the foremost expert on Sultanate India, can conclude that "by the middle of the 13th century mystic thought, both in prose and verse, had reached its finale."[3]

Yet the above judgments fail to account for the notable vitality—intellectual as well as organizational—that was generated by the fraternities. What Sufi leaders posited, on the broadest scale, was a recasting of mystic imagery and ascetical speculation in forms that could be promulgated among a wider range of people than merely the elites of Dar al-Islam. Even the impress of Imam Ghazzālī is debatable. The primary literary instrument for popularizing Sufi practises was not, as one might have expected, the Persian summaries of Ghazzālī's major tome, *Iḥyā ʿulūm ad-dīn*, but rather the Arabic handbooks, with Persian commentaries, of two Baghdadi savants, *Ādāb al-murīdīn* by Abū Najīb Suhrawardī (d. 1168) and *ʿAwārif al-maʿārif* by his nephew Abū Ḥafṣ ʿUmar Suhrawardī (d. 1234). They were not self-sufficient mystic manuals; they were intended to build on familiarity with the Qurʾān as well as knowledge of *ḥadīth.* Yet what they uniquely provided was an ideological basis for the organization of mystic life in local contexts. And they complemented the growing predilection for poetry and music that characterized most of the earliest Sufi adepts in all parts of Asia. Institutional Sufism grew because its dynamism was intellectual as well as programmatic; its originality lay in its distillation of disparate elements from the classical phase of Sufism, together with its openness to the new forms—of language, imagery and music—that emerged from the regions to which it was introduced.

Nor should one deduce that institutional Sufism, by dint of its localization, was less securely orthodox than the speculative writings of Imam Ghazzālī or other mystically minded legal scholars of his generation. J. Spencer Trimingham, whose widely cited book, *Sufi Orders in Islam*, claims to offer a historical reconstruction of Sufi brotherhoods, in fact, stakes out a thinly disguised critique of their very existence. The only true Sufism, for him, existed in the classical phase. "This development into orders, and the integral association of the saint cult with them, contributed to the decline of Sufism as a mystical Way. Spiritual insight atrophied and the Way became paved and milestoned."[4] The *ṭarīqa* phase (1100-1400) represented for Trimingham a bourgeois movement after which the decline of Sufism in the *ṭāʾifa* phase (post-1400) was inevitable.[5]

What Trimingham fails to note is the complementary function of the *silsilas*/*ṭarīqas* in the medieval Islamic world. They were not a block phenomenon with a univocal viewpoint imposed on all who joined their ranks. As Richard M. Eaton's lucid book on *Sufis of Bijapur* documents, institutionally affiliated Sufis performed a variety of functions from several motives.[6] Judgments posed in dichotomous categories, such as vibrant/decadent, creative/stagnant or orthodox/unorthodox, do not begin to allow a value-free descriptive approach to the historical evidence of the orders, yet apart from such an approach the assessment of their influence in any region of the world, including South Asia, is impossible.

It is our contention that institutional Sufism was a natural outgrowth of ascetical speculation and poetic discourse as both contributed to the stock of images gradually winnowed, refined and canonized into predictive styles of piety contrasting with, though not displacing, the public rituals of Muslim community life. The character of institutional Sufism can be most readily grasped by examing the imperious role of the leader. Whether addressed as *pīr*, *murshid* or, most frequently, *shaykh*, he was as indispensable to the fraternities as he was unacceptable to those outside them. To understand the appeal and legitimation of the fraternities is to confront the primacy of their human leaders. Neither the early Islamic community nor the classical Sufism arrogated a similar level of authority to individual men, however pious, ascetic or charismatic they may have been. The *pīr* as supreme guide in all aspects of community life is peculiar to institutional Sufism. Where did this wholesale transferal of personal authority to one man originate? Sufi tradition ascribes its genesis to Abū Saᶜīd ibn Abī l-Khayr, an eleventh-century Khorasanian master. The *pīr*'s undisputed authority is also advocated in the two guidebooks earlier mentioned, *Ādāb al-murīdīn* and *ᶜAwārif al-maᶜārif*. The author of the *Ādāb* declares: "Complete obedience and respect towards the master are required. The master in the midst of his followers is like the prophet in the midst of his community."[7] The *ᶜAwārif* is still more explicit. Its author sets forth fifteen rules of conduct which the novice is expected to observe in the presence of his Shaykh. Not only is he to have perfect faith and total obedience, but he is to relinquish all opposition, even to the point of rejecting his own will.[8] The concrete image often used by Sufis to denote the starkness of *pīr/murīd* relationship was a corpse: the disciple in the presence of his master should be like a corpse in the hands of a washerman.

Underlying this code of extreme subservience was a stratum of ontological reasoning alien to all the earliest explorations of Muslim theology (*kalām*), except perhaps Shiᶜite arguments in favor of the unique divine-human status of the Imams. The ontological status conferred upon Sufi *pīrs* has been best exposited by Marshall G. S. Hodgson in a memorable passage from his brilliant but challenging magnum opus, *The Venture of Islam*:

> Pīrs were not merely the means whereby other humans came to God. As the perfect human beings, they were the reason why the universe has been made: not merely as the specially obedient creatures of God, who give Him pleasure, but as the metaphysical goal of all the universe, including other human beings. When perfected, they were necessarily sinless, for their transformed nature was incompatible with sin (that is, separation from God) and would transform what seemed to be sin into holiness.... Indeed, a pīr could sin only by contradicting himself, the touchstone of sin in all mankind, since sin was whatever hindered people from ascending to that position in which the pīr was, and to which the pīr was the means of ascent. "Sins are made sinful by the disapproval of pīrs," Rūmī says (II, 3351), hence what a pīr (if he be true) approves cannot, by definition, be sinful.[9]

Elevation of *pīrs* to a quasi-divine status had numerous implications for the structure of institutional Sufism. One of the most significant relates to mortality: the *pīr*, by nature, not only could not sin, as Hodgson pointed out, he also could not die. To be sure, he did experience death of the body, but his spirit was presumed to live on eternally in the presence of the God whom he had served so loyally throughout his ascetical, and usually long-lived, life. As a result, the *pīr* pierced the curtain of death through the tomb which enclosed his earthly remains. He was thought to be more strongly present in that place than elsewhere, and also to be more receptive to the intercessory pleas his followers offered there on that occasion, when he came to make his departure from this life to the empyrean beyond day and night, life and death. Appropriately, that moment of celebrating the *pīr*'s triumphal passage from earth to heaven is known as *ᶜurs*, i.e., wedding ceremony: he, the lover, the bridegroom, is joined to God, the Beloved Bride, in an eternal marriage.

Though often derided as a degenerate form of pure Islam, the Sufi tomb cults embodied the logical outcome of cumulative, unbridled devotion to living saints. There was also greed involved, both on the part of relatives and hangers on, and also on the part of political/military rulers, each wanting to derive personal benefit from their special association with the deceased saint. Without greed, magnificent tombs and ancillary *masjid-madrasa* (mosque-school) complexes would never have been constructed or maintained, yet the root motive for all such attention to saintly tombs was belief, even by the greedy, in the special, even unique, importance of those who resided within the tombs.

Often there was also a network of associative saints' tombs. If a mystically minded South Asian Muslim affiliated himself with the Chishti order, for instance, he would be predisposed to attend not just one but as many as five annual *ᶜurs* ceremonies. The most important would be the anniversary celebrating the death/marriage of the saint who introduced the order to India, Muᶜīn al-Dīn Sijzī Ajmerī. He lies buried in Rajasthan. (More will be said about his cult below.) The second, fourth, and fifth saints of the same order (Quṭb al-Dīn, Niẓām al-Dīn and Naṣīr al-Dīn), all have separate tomb complexes, with different servant families and lay patrons, in one city, the capital city of Sultanate India, Delhi. Each saint has a death anniversary, and each anniversary is marked with a special celebration, of which the most extensive at present focuses on the fourth saint, Niẓām al-Dīn.[10] Only the third saint of the Chishti *silsila*, Farīd al-Dīn, lies buried elsewhere, far to the north of Delhi, in a town of the Punjab, renamed after him as Pakpattan.

Chishti lay devotees would know about the lives of the first five Chishti Shaykhs, from Muᶜīn al-Din to Naṣīr al-Dīn. They would also know the locations of their tombs, and they would know the dates for celebrating their *ᶜurs* remembrances. Hence, in the case of the Chishtiya (as well as other South Asian Sufi orders), the strength of one saint's presence and the persistence of his reputation was often reinforced by association with other saints. While the tomb cults were peculiar to each saint, the network of saints' tombs cumulatively linked Shaykh to Shaykh throughout the calendar year, decade after decade, in the minds and lives of their devotees.

Literature plays an enormous yet ambiguous role in specifying the quality of devotion accorded saints during and beyond their earthly lives. Sufis have been erratic in the way they have produced literary testimony to their heralded masters. In a mystical tradition writing is seldom upheld as the paramount vehicle of expression. Many Shaykhs, while not imposing their views on co-travelers, deliberately wrote nothing. Others wrote letters only with the caveat that they be destroyed. Still others forbade writing—and thereby invited spurious tracts purporting to be their words and thoughts. The reason for these modes of behavior is "logical," at least from a mystical viewpoint: writing is a rational rather than an intuitive endeavor. It pulls the mind down rather than lifting it up. The spoken word or silence is closer to the Absolute Truth. Also, if one does write, the reader must be a person trained to understand the significance behind words; ignorant or ill-tempered readers could misread a spiritual master's letters and literally have him hung for heresy. Yet the impulse to record, to preserve and to transmit the spiritual heritage of Sufi Shaykhs was widespread in the Muslim world, and wherever the Shaykhs themselves chose not to write, others provided the words which seemed appropriate to the life and teaching of a guide on the Path.

Within the constraints imposed by the innate prejudice against writing, four kinds of literary evidence have proved notable in the institutional phase of Sufism. One is genealogical tracts. Genealogy alone never made a single Sufi Shaykh famous, but family trees were often used by his followers as evidence to affirm that he deserved the success he achieved. There were two kinds of family trees: one pertained to the Shaykh's biological heritage, and this was particularly important to confirm him as related by blood to the earliest generations of Muslims, and perhaps even to the Prophet Muhammad himself, in which case the title "*sayyid*" could be affixed before his name. Usually, however, biological ties were subordinate to a second kind of genealogy, a spiritual genealogy that linked the Shaykh to other, already established, Sufis of earlier generations. Many of these affiliations were traced back to the tenth-century Baghdadi ascetic, Junayd. And they often overlapped. It is especially important to note that Sufi genealogies overlapped, since their tracing to early generations of Islamic adepts posited a common ancestry for the orders and gave rise to a sense of spiritual interdependency that balanced intense, seemingly exclusive loyalty to one Shaykh and to the order with which he was affiliated.

A second, recurrent kind of literature among the Sufi fraternities was frankly, shamelessly anecdotal. Sufis delighted in anecdotes on every topic—whether moral, having to do with sensual restraint and subtle codes of conduct, or miraculous, pertaining to food, procreation, conversion, and the like. Peculiar to the Shaykhs in the Asian subcontinent was a literary genre known as *malfūẓāt*. They purported to be conversations of the spiritual masters committed to writing by disciples. Their content was overwhelmingly anecdotal. Letters (*maktūbāt*) and didactic essays (*ishārāt*) shared similar traits: many points of emphasis, both complementary to and competitive with the legal/formal mandates of Islam, were often couched in anecdotes. When told by the great Shaykh, anecdotes would illustrate his authority at two levels: since he told the anecdotes, they were accepted as exemplary directives for reflection and conduct; at the same time, at a deeper level, the content of anecdotes often underscored the particular nature of one Shaykh's authority. For instance, a disciple of Muʿīn al-Dīn, the first Indian Chishti *pīr*, told the following story about his master:

> When sons had been born to Khwaja Muʿīn ad-dīn, one day he asked me: "Ḥamīd, how is it that previously, when I was young and strong, everything which I sought from God, I obtained quickly; whereas now that I have become old and weak when I pray for something which I need, there is a delay before my prayer is granted? "You know," I replied, "that before Jesus was born to Mary, without having to lift a finger, she obtained fruits in winter time and winter fruits in summer time, in her very room. After Jesus the Prophet—may God have mercy on him—was born, Mary expected to receive the same provision as before, but instead she was commanded: 'Go out and shake the trunk of the palm tree; then will it drop fresh dates on you' (Qurʾān 19:25). This is the measure of the difference between her former and her latter condition." The Khwaja accepted this answer and was pleased by it.

This story, recorded in Ḥamīd al-Dīn's conversations (*malfūẓāt*) and cited in later biographical dictionaries (*tazkiras*),[11] seemingly lauds Muʿīn al-Dīn. It is implied that he as a devout Sufi remained celibate till late in life, and only then, perhaps to fulfill the demands of Muslim law (*sharīʿa*), did he marry and father sons. Yet the anecdote also serves a second function: it lauds the scriptural knowledge and intuitive insight of the disciple who tells the story. It was Ḥamīd al-Dīn, in this instance, who knew the right Qurʾānic verse to quote to Muʿīn al-Dın; it was the disciple's answer which relieved the master's anxiety about his sagging spiritual strength.

Nor was the anecdotalism, so prevalent in Sufi literature, limited to prose. Frequently the best remembered anecdotes were those reshaped and retold in verse. It is no accident that beyond South Asia two of the supreme literary monuments of the Sufi tradition consisted primarily of versified anecdotes strung together in the poet's mind. One was the powerful allegory authored by Farīd al-Dīn ʿAṭṭār titled *Manṭiq al-ṭayr* [Bird Talk]. The birds represent numerous Sufi novices, their destination, the grandest Bird of all, whose name turns out to be, in what A. Schimmel has dubbed "the most ingenious pun in Persian literature," the collectivity of birds; i.e., it is their own selves, not some distant Other, whom they seek![12] The second, and still more famous Sufi poem, was the *Mathnavī-ye maʿnavī* of Jalāl al-Dīn Rūmī. Brilliant theologian, tireless raconteur and inventive poet, this thirteenth-century Perso-Anatolian mystic produced the most massive and exquisite distillation of ecstacy into verse in the entire history of Islam. According to Trimingham's schematization, Rūmī lived in the twilight or bourgeois period of Sufism, yet his alliterative, unsystematic, anecdotal versifications came closer to the mood of the Sufi quest than the neatly sequential, comprehensive tomes of Imam Ghazzālī 150 years earlier or even the deft, dialectical soundings of the supreme Sufi metaphysician, a near contemporary of Rūmī, Muḥyī al-Dīn ibn al-ʿArabī.

So essential was poetry to institutional Sufism that master poets were often coopted into the mystic ranks, however great may have been their distance from its rigorous personal demands. Two Shīrāzī lyricists, Saᶜdī, author of *Būstān* and *Gulistān*, and later Ḥāfiẓ, whose poetic compilation is known simply as *Dīvān-e Ḥāfiẓ*—were both revered as Sufis because the ambiguous imagery of their verse harkened to the pathos experienced by those who did travel the Path to Truth, namely, the great Shaykhs and their lay devotees.

Closely related to anecdotal narratives and poetic musings was a proclivity to music (*samāᶜ*). Like poetry, music was by nature ambivalent: it could elicit purely sensual reactions, or it could be an inducement to lift the seeker out of his customary mood, his fixed routine of responses and expectations, to a new awareness of the Divine Beloved. Few are the major poets of institutional Sufism, whether Rūmī, Saᶜdī or Ḥāfiẓ, who were not advocates of spiritual music and participants in assemblies where music and also dance were enjoyed by like-minded Sufi brethren. Most of the major Sufi theoreticians, from Imam Ghazzālī to the Suhrawardīs to Sharaf al-Dīn Manerī (a Bihari Shaykh of wide renown),[13] advocated at least limited participation in musical assemblies at the outset of the mystic quest. Such gatherings did provoke antagonism with the *ᶜulamāʾ*, those learned functionaries, educators and jurists who conducted ritual prayer and ordered public life, but rather than weaken the commitment of the Sufi masters to music, antagonism with the *ᶜulamāʾ* seems to have intensified their defense of its usage. Especially in regions of the world where Islamization had barely begun by the thirteenth century, Sufi Shaykhs gambled that through their charisma, their devoted followers and their convivial ceremonies, including musical assemblies, they would attract greater attention, sympathy and support than the sincere but dull, educated but aloof *ᶜulamāʾ*.[14] Their gamble succeeded, at least up through the mid-sixteenth century when large-scale military patronage states emerged in Turkey, Iran and India, changing the profile of the medieval Muslim world as well as the function of Sufi orders within it.

Neither music nor poetry nor anecdotalism nor genealogical tabulations determined the success of individual Sufi Shaykhs. Taken together, however, they comprised a pattern of piety that was distinctive to institutional Sufism. Even though some features, such as anecdotalism, had been incipiently present in the classical phase of Sufism, each developed in a particular way to magnify the cult of the *pīr*.

It is the posthumous function of saints' cults which is essential to understanding local contexts and yet has been understudied with reference to them. Saints' cults were not invariably consistent in tenor with the teaching or example of the venerated, deceased master. Many of them, in fact, seem to have functioned in a manner antithetical to the doctrines and deeds of the saint resident in their cultic tomb. Should we then conclude peremptorily that posthumous cults rather than actual saints' lives are the source of what Anawati calls "degeneracy," Trimingham, "the paved Way"? With respect to Indian Islam the case is weak; available evidence does not admit of a judgment that can be either inclusive in scope or categorical in tone. Each evaluation depends on regional factors, biographical patterns, and circumstances shaping the formation of individual cults.

Institutional Sufism in Rajasthan, Gujarat and Kashmir

To indicate the variability of institutional Sufism as it functioned on the periphery of Dar al-Islam we have selected three regions in South Asia that are seldom analyzed as discrete geographic entities, with independent social and religious histories, especially during the pre-modern period: Rajasthan, Gujarat and Kashmir.

Medieval Rajasthan was strategically crucial because it bridged coastal Gujarat and interior commercial/administrative centers, not the least of which was Delhi. It was militarily powerful because its indigenous tribal elites, loosely known as Rajputs, were hardened mountain warriors with a keen sense of social solidarity. Among important cities in medieval Rajasthan were Ajmer and Nagor, though Ajmer, as capital of the region, enjoyed a longstanding preeminence. It was hardly coincidental, therefore, that the first—and some would say, the foremost—Shaykh of the major Sultanate Sufi order, the Chishtiya, chose to settle in Ajmer.

The actual data we have about Muᶜīn al-Dīn Sijzī Chishtī Ajmerī is very slim. It may be summarized as follows:[15] **a.** he was born and lived in Sijistan; hence he bore the *nisba* (after-name) of Sijzī; **b.** he joined the discipline of the Chishti Shaykh, ᶜUthmān Harwanī, and became his principal *khalīfa* or successor; **c.** he traveled to Delhi, undoubtedly after visiting some major centers of the Muslim world, but which, when and with what outcome inclear; **d.** he arrived at Ajmer around the time of its conquest by the Turkish army officer and early Indian Sultan, Shihāb al-Dīn Ghorī (d. 1206); **e.** he had two major disciples, Ḥamīd al-Dīn Sawalī and Quṭb al-Dīn Bakhtiyār Kākī; the latter became his principal disciple, though the means of exchange is uncertain; **f.** he died in 1233 in Ajmer, where he was buried in a modest tomb.

Less important than this skeletal biography, however, is the operative image, admittedly hagiographic, of Muᶜīn al-Dīn. It includes all the four elements cited above as central to the depiction of a Sufi Shaykh in his role as unquestioned leader of a mystical order or movement. The genealogy of Muᶜīn al-Dīn is refined in both dimensions, biological and spiritual. Though we don't know his exact pedigree, we are led to believe, by inference, that he was a *sayyid* from accounts of his marriage, late in life, to a young *sayyida*, Bībī ᶜIṣmat, whose father was very concerned that she marry "properly," i.e., marry another *sayyid.* (By contrast, Muᶜīn al-Dīn's second wife, Amatullāh, was apparently not a *sayyida*, which led to disputes over the parentage of Muᶜīn al-Dīn's three sons, all of whom, to have qualified as pure *sayyid*s, would have had to have been the issue of Muᶜīn al-Dīn and Bībī ᶜIṣmat.)

For the mass of his devotees, however, it is the spiritual genealogy of the saint from Ajmer which far outweighs his blood line or that of his offspring. It is traceable to earlier pre-Indian Chishti Shaykhs and ultimately back to an eighth-century Sufi leader, Ḥasan al-Baṣrī. The genealogy is bolstered by anecdotes, some of which include recollection of meetings Muᶜīn al-Dīn had with other leading Shaykhs before his arrival in India. (All of them, not surprisingly, confirmed the high spiritual station Muᶜīn al-Dīn had reached, and the unique Islamic mission he was to carry out in Hindustan.) Other anecdotes alluded to the extraordinary proclivity of the Chishti standard bearer to *samāᶜ*, that is, to music sung in mystical assemblies. One popular story even attributes Muᶜīn al-Dīn's success as an Islamic proselytizer to his espousal of *samāᶜ*. Moreover, lyrical verses, enough to comprise a thin *dīvān* (poetic compilation) have also been attributed to Muᶜīn al-Dīn, and continue to be recited among his devotees as part of the saint's spiritual legacy.

Further attestations to Muᶜīn al-Dīn's status as a Sufi exemplar and divine intercessor are manifest in the enormous *dargāh* complex at Ajmer, for which his canopied tomb is the central ritual object. It might be argued that the strategic significance of Rajasthan in general and Ajmer in particular led the saint to settle there, even as it determined the posthumous success of his cult. Following this line of interpretation, one could minimize the free choice of every actor related to the Ajmeri cult, from the mendacious *dīvāns* who engage in legal hassles over biological genealogy to Akbar the Great, the arch-Mughal dynast who journeyed there on his knees after being granted a boon he attributed to the saint's intercession; all of them could be seen as having been motivated by culturally conditioned modes of behavior, in this case, the expectation of divine mediation through saintly tombs, the resting places of deceased Sufi Shaykhs. Yet there is also an arguable element of historical happenstance or random occurrence in the development of the Ajmer cult. From an early period the *dargāh* complex attracted non-Muslim as well as Muslim adherents. In the British period it withstood the desacralization of colonial administrators in Rajasthan, and in the present century it survived the miltilayered assaults of Partition. Not all tomb cults have fared so well. Why? Several historical factors, both literary and systemic, provide clues, but they do not constitute absolute indices predictive of a certain outcome. For the devotee, happenstance is "divine favor"; for the historian, it is that random occurrence for which no tangible, verifiable cause can be reasonably surmised. Either way it has to be allowed in considering the evidence of tomb cults.

In some cases the failure of a tomb cult—or more precisely, the minimalization of its public ritual and *dargāh* improvement program—was intentional. Yet is it not also, at least in part, a matter of historical happenstance that intentional modesty could be maintained, rather than yielding to the impetus for expansion that has characterized Ajmer and other "successful" Sufi cult centers?

One notable example of a deliberately unsuccessful tomb cult also occurs in the Rajasthani context. Muᶜīn al-Dīn's second major disciple, Ḥamīd al-Dīn Sawalī Nāgorī, (d. 1274) settled in a rural area of Rajasthan. There he earned his living as a farmer Sufi (in contrast to Muᶜīn al-Dīn, and most other

Chishti Shaykhs, who lived off the charitable donations of their devotees in urban centers). Despite his physical labors, Ḥamīd al-Dīn wrote—letters, poems, essays, prayers. We have a sizable, authentic literary legacy from this thirteenth-century Rajasthani agriculturalist. It includes an impassioned defense of *samā*ᶜ, mystic music, to which he and his descendants were unshakably attached. The epistle on *samā*ᶜ, numerous verses and abundant anecdotes about the farmer saint from Nagor, including the one earlier cited about Muᶜīn al-Dīn's perplexity at his postmarital loss of spiritual power—all are included in an enormous *malfūẓāt* (collection of his conversations) compiled by one of his grandchildren.[16]

Ḥamīd al-Dīn's familial or biological genealogy is slightly less exalted than Muᶜīn al-Dīn's. He was a *shaykh* rather than a *sayyid*, that is to say, his family traced its descent from one of the companions of the Prophet Muḥammad. Yet unlike Muᶜīn al-Dīn, Ḥamīd ad-dīn was actually a native South Asian; by his own testimony, he was the first child born into a Muslim family after the conquest of Delhi. On a spiritual plane, Ḥamīd al-Dīn's genealogy matches Muᶜīn al-Dīn's, since he adopts the same mystical forebears as his *pīr*, tracing his "real" ancestry back to Ḥasan al-Baṣrī.

Despite these impressive credentials—both ascriptive and achieved—the tomb cult of Ḥamīd al-Dīn never flourished. During the Mughal period, when the complex of Muᶜīn al-Dīn underwent its first major development, few changes were made in the Nagor shrine, even though prominent members of the Mughal court, including Abu l-Faẓl, Akbar the Great's principal biographer, were themselves former residents of Nagor and did direct imperial patronage to other parts of their native city. The successors to Ḥamīd al-Dīn, who have tended his tomb and perpetuated his cult to the present day, have extolled rather than lamented its meagre artifacts. Proudly they have claimed to have honored the Sufi dictum; *faqrī fakhrī* (my poverty is my pride). Whatever the reason (conscious avoidance abetted by historical circumstance?), there can be no doubt that the saint who was humble, poor and regional continues to lie buried in a tomb site that mirrors these same qualities, its only adornment being an impressive gate that a fourteenth-century Delhi sultan insisted on building over the objections of the tomb custodians.

The pan-Indian network of the Chishti *silsila* does partially impinge on the Nagor cult. While the major lines of succession from Muᶜīn al-Dīn go through another disciple, Quṭb al-Dīn (who lived in Delhi), rather than through Ḥamīd al-Dīn, spiritual pedigrees do overlap from time to time: some later Chishti Shaykhs trace their ancestry through Ḥamīd al-Dīn as well as through Quṭb al-Dīn back to Muᶜīn al-Dīn and all his non-Indian forebears. One such saint is Khwāja Khānū, a sixteenth-century Sufi leader from Gwaliyor. He lies buried in a tomb shrine which, like that of Ḥamīd al-Dīn, is a deliberate understatement of its resident's spiritual prowess.

In sum, Rajasthan provides ample testimony to a double profile for Sufi cults in the subcontinent—high for Muᶜīn al-Dīn in Ajmer, low for Ḥamīd al-Dīn in Nagor. Regional factors and biographical patterns largely explain this disjuncture, but allowance for historical circumstance or random occurrence must also be made in trying to sum up the net result of six centuries of evolution.

Gujarat is a low-lying coastal region to the southwest of Rajasthan bordering the Arabian Sea. Because of its continuous access to overseas trade, its sundry Muslim-Hindu commercial guilds, and its diverse linguistic, ethnic and cultural traditions, Gujarat attests to a still more varied pattern of development for institutional Sufism than does Rajasthan. Like Rajasthan, its most prominent saint cults were linked to the period when Islam was introduced to the area, but unlike Rajasthan, the deceased Shaykhs whose remains and relics were venerated in Gujarat belonged to regional orders of restricted popularity, e.g., the Maghribi and Shaṭṭari, or to pan-Islamic orders important in the Arab world, e.g., the Suhrawardi.

Despite these differences, the pivotal biographical features of Gujarati Sufi masters, as they were elaborated and transmitted through posthumous cults, concerned genealogy and anecdotes (to a lesser extent, poetry and music), as they had in Rajasthan. There are, however, Gujarati sites where saint cults developed apart from the biographical/hagiographical pattern outlined above. Their ultimate fate would seem to underscore the necessity for attention to a sustainable, charismatic profile linked to the resident of a major tomb site. Negatively, they confirm our thesis that biographical data does matter in the evolution of succesful saint cults in South Asia.

Consider the case of Sarkhej. It was once a splendid resort city outside Ahmadabad. There lies buried the most acclaimed of all pre-Mughal Gujarati Shaykhs, Aḥmad Khattū (d. 1445). His mausoleum was constructed by Sultan Muḥammad Shāh, oldest son of Ahmadabad's founder, Aḥmad Shāh, in 1446. Unlike Ajmer and Nagor, there is not only a *mazār* but an elaborate mosque and imposing *madrasa* all located within the same compound. Dominating a pond that was cleared to highlight its location is the broad dome beneath which was built the glittering marbled canopy of Aḥmad Khattū. Gujarat's two most renowned sultans lie buried just beyond this domed edifice, as it were at the feet of Aḥmad Khattū, in far less imposing tombs: Sultan Maḥmūd Begada (1458-1511) and Sultan Muẓaffar II (1511-26).

Yet the cult of Aḥmad Khattū had declined to a local affair of limited appeal even before the British established permanent rule in Ahmadabad during the early nineteenth century. Why? At least a partial cause is the saint's underdeveloped biographical profile. His genealogy is obscure: the generational tree (*shajra*) of his biological family is not reported because he was orphaned at an early age. Nor are his spiritual ancestry and progeny remarkable: heir to a *silsila* (the Maghribi) which boasts no other major Shaykh in the subcontinent, he did not, in turn, produce a pan-Indian or even a regionally significant group of disciples to perpetuate his fame. Anecdotes about him do exist, but they are recorded in *malfūẓāt* of mediocre literary value. There are few, very few anecdotes indicating his taste for music and limited appreciation of poetry.[17]

Contrasting with Aḥmad Khattū in the durative popularity of his tomb cult is a Gujarati Shaykh frequently linked to him as a "brother" Sufi. Sayyid Burhān al-Dīn Quṭb-i ᶜAlam Bukhārī (d. 1453), as his very name reflects, was biologically descended from the family of the Prophet Muḥammad. He had the further distinction of being spiritually as well as biologically related to the famed Punjabi saint, Sayyid Jalāl al-Dīn Bukhārī Makhdūm-i Jahāniyān Jahāngasht (d. 1384), himself fourth in line of descent from the founder of the Suhrawardi order, Abū Ḥafṣ ᶜUmar Suhrawardī (d. 1234). Contemporary and subsequent literature extols the virtues of Burhān al-Dīn as a Sufi exemplar, even though there is no indication that the *sayyid* penned poetry or was especially prone to participate in fraternal music assemblies (*maḥāfil-e samāᶜ*). His tomb shrine, like that of Aḥmad Khattū, was initially built from the charitable donation of a local ruler, the same Sulṭān Aḥmad Shāh (1411-1441), who had befriended Aḥmad Khattū and whose son, Sulṭān Muḥammad Shāh (1442-1449), had ordered the construction of Khattū's tomb. Yet the two shrines are not comparable: Aḥmad Khattū's shrine far outshines that of his contemporary brother Sufi from the Suhrawardī order.

Why then did Burhān al-Dīn's tomb enjoy a more sustained cultic fame than Aḥmad Khattū's? The contrast in their genealogical attributions is an insufficient explanation. Instead, one must investigate historical developments deriving from the interaction of biographical patterns and ritual needs. Preliminarily, it should be noted that in neither case does the fame of the saint's shrine extend beyond Gujarat, or indeed beyond the network of villages and towns linked to Ahmadabad, the capital city of that prosperous, mercantile state. Burhān al-Dīn's tomb, like Muᶜīn al-Dīn's in Ajmer, indicates the way in which cults may take on a life of their own, independent of or only loosely derived from the character of their saintly resident. Located at Batva, a suburb of Ahmadabad, the tomb-hospice complex of Burhān al-Dīn continues to attract large numbers of devotees to monthly as well as annual celebrations on behalf of the Bukhari *sayyid*. A major part of the attraction is a rock, the mysterious rock of Batva. It is said to be a unique admixture of lead, iron and wood "revealed" to Burhān al-Dīn as proof of his spiritual attainments.[18] Hindus of various classes and backgrounds join with the Muslim servants and client families at Batva to honor Burhān al-Dīn's rock, and also to derive benefits from it. There is no recorded history of how the ceremony of revering the Batva rock began, but as celebrated at present, it suggests a shamanistic ritual with Muslim markings and bicreedal participants.

Literary evidence indicates that the rock played a minor role in the actual life and the earliest biographies of Burhān al-Dīn. Through the posthumous development of his cult, however, the rock at some now lost point in time became the major object symbolizing the saint's spiritual prowess and ensuring the perpetuation of his memory among Ahmadabad's inhabitants. Other factors, including the variant development of Batva and Sarkhej as adjunct communities to Ahmadabad during the late Mughal and early modern period, undoubtedly contributed to the disparity between the two tomb cults of Aḥmad

Khattū and Burhān al-Dīn. Yet without the rock at Batva it seems fair to conclude that both would have suffered the same precipitous decline.

A third Gujarati shrine has become still more mute at the present day than Aḥmad Khattū's. The case is ironic because of the dramatic degree to which it reverses the expected causes of saintly acclaim. If literary artifacts, rather than genealogical purity, anecdotal associations, poetic and/or musical affinities, were the primary determinent of a deceased saint's perdurable fame, the most illustrious saint of Gujarat should have been Shāh Wajīh al-Dīn ᶜAlavī (d. 1589). The biography of Wajīh al-Dīn reads like a *madrasa adab* manual on how to be a perfect Muslim. It is far more factual and detailed, at least in form, than that of either Aḥmad Khattū or Burhān ad-Dīn. A *ḥāfiẓ* and a *muqriʾ* (Qurʾān memorizer and reciter) at the age of seven, he also mastered *tafsīr* (commentary), *ḥadīth*, *fiqh* (law), *naḥw* (grammar), *manṭiq* (logic), *falsafa* (philosophy), and *kalām* (theology) by early adolescence. So comprehensive and prolific was his subsequent scholarship that Badāʾūnī, the renowned Mughal historian, could say of him: "There was hardly a standard work from the treatises on the accidental property of light to books of law and medicine ... which he had not annotated and adorned with a commentary."[19] Moreover, in daily dress and conduct, Wajīh al-Dīn was said to have been a true Sufi, clothing himself in the coarse garments made fashionable by ninth-century Iraqi ascetics, at the same time that he held audience with all classes of people in sixteenth-century Ahmadabad.

Even the mystical affiliations of Shāh Wajīh al-Dīn should have endeared him to future generations of Hindus as well as Muslims. He was a major disciple of Muḥammad Ghaws̱ Gwaliyarī (d. 1563), author of *Jawāhir al-khamsa*, in the most syncretistic of all medieval Sufi orders, the Shaṭṭariya. Yet his biographical profile is deficient in all these elements outlined as essential to a successful saint cult: genealogically he was linked to Shiᶜite Islam, anecdotes about him are sparse, his taste for poetry and music negligible. Is it any surprise then that the tomb-hospice-*madrasa* complex of Wajīh al-Dīn built at Khanpur in the center of Ahmadabad, but a short distance from the spacious and elegant Jāmiᶜ Masjid (cathedral mosque), suffered an eclipse by the end of the eighteenth century, even before the British occupation was forcefully felt at all levels of society? At present only Wajīh al-Dīn's tomb is extant. It is a piteous reminder of better times. The memory of the extraordinary scholar-saint whom it encloses is kept alive only by Wajīh al-Dīn's urbane, wealthy and politically active descendants.

One could conclude that the fate of Gujarat's Muslim saint shrines has been determined as much by the history of that province as by biographical patterns or cultic developments. Gujarati tombs, like Gujarat itself, have been relatively isolated from the mainstream of events that affected North India's Turco-Muslim elite. While Rajasthan is geographically proximate to northern cities such as Delhi, the central metropolis of Muslim India, Gujarat is coastal, its overseas trade linking it as much to foreign Muslim communities as to those located in interior India. Hence, Rajasthani saints tended to belong to pan-

India *silsilas* and to attract adherents from several regions of the subcontinent. Gujarat, on the other hand, produced saints whose fame was not only regionalized but often purely local. Yet *within* Gujarat, biographical patterns (or their absence, particularly in the case of Aḥmad Khattū and Wajīh al-Dīn ᶜAlavī) as well as cultic developments (for example, the rock at Batva) did influence the extent and duration of a saint's local fame.

In ways not readily discernible, all the saints so far examined were beneficiaries of regional loyalty, even as they, in turn, helped to intensify area-specific, corporate identity particularly through the posthumous development of their tomb cults. Is it not possible, however, that the too focused regional loyalties of his followers might restrict a saint whose contemporary reputation, *silsila* affiliation and tomb cult qualified him for pan-Indian fame? Such appears to have been the case with Sayyid ᶜAlī Hamadānī (d. 1385), the most renowned saint of pre-Mughal Kashmir. The *sayyid*'s name is inextricably linked with the advent of Islam to one of the most remote but beautiful regions of the subcontinent.

In a sense, medieval Kashmir was like medieval Gujarat. It was a territory beyond the military conquest, and hence the administrative control, of the Delhi Sultans. Also like Gujarat (but unlike Rajasthan), it did not enter the Mughal fold except after a tenacious struggle and at a comparatively late date (1586).

Yet Kashmir is perhaps even more obdurate than Gujarat to centralizing forces such as those which shaped the nascent Islamic polity in the subcontinent. Kashmir is a valley. The valley cannot be easily invaded nor quickly subjugated. Inhabitants of the valley yield to non-indigenous cultural forms slowly, grudingly, in most cases by transforming them into something identified as "Kashmiri."

Sayyid ᶜAlī Hamadānī, before coming to Srinagar in 1379, had been a well-born, widely traveled Central Asian Muslim scholar-saint. He lived in Srinagar for less than five years and died while on a trip to Kunar in the northwest, from whence he was removed to Khatlan in presentday Tajikistan for burial. Around the site of his hospice (*khānaqāh*) in Srinagar was built a towering wood framed mosque, which continues to serve as both a place of prayer and a center of pilgrimage for Kashmiri Muslims. Two features of the Sayyid's life and cult are especially relevant to this essay. One concerns his biography. Tradition has it that the venerable Shaykh came to the alley with 700 disciples and that the inhabitants, under the influence of this benign assault, embraced Islam. More plausible is the following: that the *sayyid* from Hamadan established a network of affiliated Shaykhs who perpetuated his teaching so well that, despite frequent opposition (to which veiled reference can be found even in the hagiographic literature of his followers), he was seen retrospectively to have converted the populace of the valley to Islam.[20] In other words, the cult of ᶜAlī Hamadānī modified his biography, though in a direction that appears to have been consonant with the aims and teachings of the saint.

The second feature which concerns us is ʿAlī Hamadānī's *silsila* and the limitation of its influence. The Sayyid belonged to the Kubravi order. No other saint from this *silsila* gained renown in the vast area of South Asia beyond Kashmir, even though the Firdausiya, prominent in Bihar, branched off from the Kubrawiya and certain saints of other *silsila*s, such as ʿAlī's alleged traveling companion, Sayyid Ashraf Jahāngīr Simnānī (d. 1428), had originally been Kubrawi.[21] It was soley within Kashmir at minor centers, such as Rostabazar, Vathi and Pattan, all of them affiliated to the Srinagar shrine, that the *Sayyid*'s teachings and writings were disseminated. Yet his genealogy, both biological and spiritual, was impeccable; his literary legacy, including anecdotal data of several varieties, was enormous; his proclivity to poetry, evidenced in a thin *dīvān*; his enjoyment of Qurʾānic chanting (and perhaps also Kashmiri music), amply attested. Why did this remarkable saint, with a panoply of charms and skills, not find a wider audience in the community of South Asian Muslims?

The answer, in our view, lies not in the avowed intent of tomb custodians (as was partially the case with Ṣūfī Ḥamīd al-Dīn Nāgorī) but in the nature of Kashmir. Because Sayyid ʿAlī was identified with Kashmiri Islam, neither he nor his disciples nor his spiritual legacy were exportable to other regions of the subcontinent. In death, even more than in life, Sayyid ʿAlī Hamadānī became as isolated as the valley which, on the putative impress of a mere five years' residence, claimed him as its first, its unique, its enduring Sufi exemplar.

The proprietary zest of Kashmiri devotionalism is further confirmed in the Rishī order. Its founder, Nūr al-Dīn, was a native-born Kashmiri. The dates of his birth are uncertain, but it has been alleged that he was seven years old at the time of Sayyid ʿAlī's death in 1385.[22] There is scant likelihood that the two men knew each other, much less were influenced by a common Sufi teaching, especially since Nūr al-Dīn's verses reflect folk Śaivism more than any version of *taṣawwuf*. Yet because Sayyid ʿAlī Hamadānī and Nūr al-Dīn Rishī enjoyed enormous fame in Kashmir, the two have been linked together through descendents of Sayyid ʿAlī in the popular, local lore of the valley, and Nūr al-Dīn's Rishi followers, like Hamadānī's Kubravi disciples, have never flourished beyond the skein of mountains and vales that comprise Kashmir.

Conclusion

To conclude is to restate the ambiguity of historical patterns evolving from the localization of Sufi orders in the Asian subcontinent. There can be no doubt that widespread devotion to living saints and also to tomb edifices containing deceased saints characterized the spiritual outlook—Geertz' now famous "moods, motivations and ritual actions"—of many South Asian Muslims, both elites and nonelites. Yet there is no single pattern for local contextualization in South Asian Islam. The three regions we examined evolved variant and distinct ethnic-linguistic-social markings that characterized all aspects of their corporate life. In particular, geographical-tactical proximity to the urban centers of ruling elites shaped much of the response to outside groups, including Sufi orders. A region such as Rajasthan was molded by its historic interconnection with Muslim Delhi, just as Gujarat and Kashmir were exceptionalized by their distance from the same urban political-administrative center of North India.

Within the Sufi orders, too, there were differences in the manner of their accomodation to local contexts. In some cases the same order could exhibit both an interface of biography and cult, doctrine and organization, as was the case with Ḥamīd al-Dīn Nāgorī, or a glaring contradiction, as was the case with Muᶜīn al-Dīn Ajmerī. The four crucial components for a biographical/doctrinal base from which could develop a successful saint's cult were: genealogical purity, anecdotally studded popularity, and proclivites to poetry as well as music. For those saints, such as Wajīh al-Dīn ᶜAlavī and Aḥmad Khattū Maghribī, in whose recollected biographies some or all of these elements have been weak and occasionally absent, the resulting cults have not survived till the modern period, though one must also acknowledge that there are places (such as Ajmer and Nagor) where random occurrences have amplified or impeded predictable cultic developments.

Finally, it ought to be noted that due to the very nature of the evolution of saints' cults the most famous shrines do not invariably house the most worthy Shaykhs. (Would it not be difficult to argue, for instance, that Muᶜīn al-Dīn deserves to be more highly touted than Ḥamīd al-Dīn?) Moreover, contemporary histories of South Asian Islam, to the extent that they tend to rely on the literary data of urban centers, have often neglected to emphasize outstanding saints' cults from peripheral regions, such as Burhān al-Dīn Bukhārī of Batva and Sayyid ᶜAlī Hamadānī of Srinagar.

NOTES

1 G. Anawati, "Philosophy, Theology and Mysticism" in J. Schacht and C. E. Bosworth, eds., *The Legacy of Islam*, (2d ed.; Oxford: Oxford University Press, 1974), p. 368.

2 Anawati, "Philosophy," p. 379.

3 K. A. Nizami, *Some Aspects of Religion and Politics in India during the Thirteenth Century* (2d ed.; Delhi: Idārah-i Adabīyat-i Delli, 1974), p. 56.

4 J. Spencer Trimingham, *The Sufi Orders in Islam* (Oxford: Oxford University Press, 1971), p. 70.

5 Timingham, *Sufi Orders*, p. 102.

6 R. M. Eaton, *Sufis of Bijapur 1300-1700: Social Roles of Sufis in Medieval India* (Princeton: Princeton University Press, 1978), especially pp. 283-96.

7 M. Milson, trans., *A Sufi Rule for Novices: Kitāb Ādāb al-Murīdīn of Abū al-Najīb al-Suhrawardī* (Cambridge & London: Harvard University Press, 1975), p. 46.

8 ᶜAbd al-Qāhir b. ᶜAbdallāh al-Suhrawardī, *Kitāb ᶜAwārif al-Maᶜārif* (Beirut: Dār al-Kitāb al-ᶜArabī, 1966), pp. 403-13.

9 Marshall G. S. Hodgson, *The Venture of Islam: Conscience and History in a World Civilization*, 3 vols. (Chicago: The University of Chicago Press, 1974), vol. 2, p. 252.

10 For an exhaustive treatment of the shrine cults surrounding the first five Chishti Shaykhs of North India, see Simon Digby, "*Tabarrukāt* and Succession among the Great Chishti Shaykhs of the Delhi Sultanate," forthcoming in R. E. Frykenberg, ed., *Delhi Through the*

Ages: Studies in Urban Culture and Society (papers presented in honor of Sir T. G. Percival Spear at an Indian History Seminar-Workshop, University of Wisconsin at Madison, Oct. 31-Nov. 1, 1979).

11 First cited in Farīd al-Dīn Nāgorī, *Surūr al-ṣudūr* [see fn. 16 below] the anecdote was later quoted by ᶜAbd al-Ḥaqq Muḥaddith Dihlavī, *Akhbār al-akhyār* (Delhi: Maṭbaᶜ-e Muḥammadī, 1283/1866), pp. 111-12.

12 Annemarie Schimmel, *Mystical Dimensions of Islam* (Chapel Hill: The University of North Carolina Press, 1975) p. 307. The mythical Bird whom the other birds seek is the Sīmurgh, and since there are thirty (*sī*) restless, searching birds (*murgh/murghān*), the reader, like the birds, is gradually led to realize that *sī* + *murgh* = Sīmurgh.

13 Sharaf ad-Dīn is now being rediscovered, his importance highlighted, through the diligent research of Paul Jackson. See Jackson's translation of *Maktūbāt-e Sadī*: Sharafuddin Maneri. *The Hundred Letters* (New York: The Paulist Press, 1980), especially Letter 93 (pp. 382-93) on *samāᶜ*.

14 Any generalization is subject to exceptions, and in medieval India there were also *ᶜulamāʾ* whose sincerity as teachers and *éclat* as preachers made them natural allies of the Sufi Shaykhs. Examples of such inspirational *ᶜulamāʾ* abound in the *malfūẓāt* and *taẕkira* literature; note K. A. Nizami, *op. cit.*, pp. 150-73.

15 Contemporary understanding of both Muᶜīn al-Dīn and his cult has been greatly enhanced by P. M. Currie's detailed study: "The Shrine and Cult of Muᶜīn al-Dīn Chishtī of Ajmer," (diss., Oxford University, 1978). I have paraphrased some of Currie's major points in the brief passages relating to Muᶜīn al-Dīn in the present essay.

16 *Surūr al-ṣudūr*, as the *malfūẓāt* of Ḥamīd al-Dīn is titled, has never been edited or published. It is a comparatively rare manuscript, of which one excellent copy exists in the Ḥabīb Ganj of Maulānā Āzād Library, Aligarh Muslim University, India, and another apparently in the manuscript collection of the University of the Punjab, Lahore, Pakistan (see Iḥsān al-Ḥaqq Fārūqī, *Sulṭān al-tārikīn* (Karachi: Dāʾira-ye Muᶜīn al-Maᶜārif, 1383/1963), *passim*).

17 For a detailed exposition of Aḥmad Khattū's checkered life, see K. A. Nizami, "Shaykh Aḥmad Maghribī as a Great Historical Personality of Medieval Gujarat" in *Medieval India—a Miscellany* (Bombay: Asia Publishing House; vol. 3, 1975), pp. 234-59. The same article has been partially summarized, without acknowledgement, in S. A. A. Rizvi, *A History of Indian Sufism* (Delhi: Munshiram Manoharlal; vol. 1, 1978), pp. 404-408.

18 ᶜAbd al-Ḥaqq, *Akhbār al-akhyār*, p. 156. ᶜAbd al-Ḥaqq also notes (pp. 156-57) that the development of interest in *samāᶜ* as a major feature of the Gujarati branch of the Suhrawardiya began with Burhān al-Dīn's son, Sayyid Muḥammad Shāh-i ᶜĀlam (d. 1475).

19 W. Haig, trans., ᶜAbd al-Qādir Badāʾūnī's *Muntakhab al-tavārīkh* (Calcutta: Bibliotheca Indica; Part 3, 1925), p. 70. The passage has also been cited in M. A. Quraishi, *Muslim Education and Learning in Gujarat (1297-1758)* (Baroda: University of Baroda Press, 1972), p. 220.

20 From a Sufi perspective, however, this point is moot, for it presupposes a calendric, multicausal view of human actions and historical events. Since the disciples trained by Sayyid ᶜAlī would have ascribed to him all their spiritual power and influence, he *did*, in their view, convert the valley of Kashmir to Islam, no matter how the story is told.

21 Concerning the Firdausiya and Sayyid ᶜAshraf Jahāngīr Simnānī, see B. Lawrence, *Notes from a Distant Flute: Sufi Literature in pre-Mughal India* (London & Tehran: Imperial Iranian Academy of Philosophy, 1978), pp. 53, 72, 100.

22 The confusing quasi-historical references to the near contemporaneity of the two Kashmiri saints have been briefly charted in A. Q. Rafiqi, *Sufism in Kashmir from the Fourteenth to the Sixteenth Century* (Varanasi: Bharatiya Publishing House, n.d.), pp. 142-43.

Contributions to Asian Studies, Vol. XVII

Court of Man, Court of God

Local Perceptions of the Shrine of Bābā Farīd, Pakpattan, Punjab

RICHARD M. EATON
University of Arizona, Tucson, Arizona, U.S.A.

IN HIS RECENT BOOK *The Cult of the Saints*, Peter Brown has discussed how, between the third and the sixth centuries, a Christian cult of saints—the "invisible friends in invisible places," as he calls them—grew up in the great cemeteries that lay outside the cities of the Roman world. The tombs of these saints were privileged places, Brown wrote, precisely because they were considered places "where the contrasted poles of Heaven and Earth met," for "the saint in Heaven was believed to be 'present' at his tomb on earth."[1] In this sense, the world of Christian late antiquity, argued Brown, can be seen as a reversal of classical Greek thought, in which the boundaries, between gods and humans were firm and unbridgeable. With the rise of the cult of the saints, such boundaries melted away.

Looking at post-thirteenth century Islam as it expanded outside its Arabic-speaking heartland, one finds a strikingly similar phenomenon. Here, too, there arose a cult of the saints—many cults, actually—which had the effect of softening if not erasing the stark boundary separating Heaven and Earth as posited by Islam in its formal or legalistic sense. Many scholars of Islamic civilization have made this observation in a general way. But what has been lacking is any careful study of how Islam after the thirteenth century was mediated to whole societies and sustained by any one of these tomb cults and, above all, how Islam and the cult were viewed from the local perspective, that is, by those believers who were integrated into the religious and social world of one of these shrines.

The aim of this paper is to address just this topic by analyzing the local perceptions of devotees of the shrine of Ḥazrat Farīd al-Dīn Ganj-i Shakar, a thirteenth-century Sufi whose tomb and shrine are located in the town of Pakpattan, in Pakistani Punjab. Popularly known simply as Bābā Farīd, this saint has remained for many centuries an immensely popular "invisible friend" among millions of villagers who have inhabited the southwestern Punjab.

Just as the immediate beneficiaries of legal disputes are lawyers, historians are perhaps the ultimate beneficiaries of such disputes. In December, 1934, Saᶜīd Muḥammad, who was the religious head of the shrines of Bābā Farīd, died, leaving behind him his eleven-year-old son, Quṭb al-Dīn, as his chosen successor for his position. Only four months later, however, a local group of devotees at the shrine, who like Saᶜīd Muḥammad were genealogical descendants of Bābā Farīd, filed a legal plaint in the nearby District Court in which they not only disputed Quṭb al-Dīn's claim to the shrine's leadership, but substituted a rival claimant, Ghulām Rasūl, for this post. In order to fortify their respective cases, lawyers for both sides of the dispute solicited the testimony of a large number of the shrine's devotees, most of them common villagers, as to their views of the shrine's religious practices. Between April 6, 1935 when Ghulām Rasūl filed his plaint, and December 2, 1938 when a District Court judge decided the case in favor of the defendant, Quṭb al-Dīn, no less than 159 oral depositions were filed on behalf of the plaintiff and 172 on behalf of the defendant, covering in all over 836 typed pages. In addition, both sides filed nearly three hundred documents with the Court. As a body, the depositions, submitted for the most part by local peasant-devotees from the districts of Montgomery (now Sahiwal), Bahawalpur and Lyallpur, provide a remarkable sampling of the shrine's local constituency, documenting how the latter viewed the shrine's relationship to God, to Islamic Law, to the British government that ultimately ruled them, and to their own daily lives. As such, they afford an intimate look at how Islam, as sustained and mediated by this shrine, was popularly perceived in one locality of the Muslim world.[2]

The Shrine and the Exchange of Religious Goods

In the minds of his many devotees, called *murīds*, Bābā Farīd was an "invisible friend" not only to them; he was also a "friend of God," or *walī*. It is in this capacity to serve as a friend both of god and of the *murīd*, to join as it were the opposing poles of Heaven and Earth, that we see the basic religious role not only of Bābā Farīd, but also of his shrine and its religious leader. Called the *sajjāda-nishīn*, *gaddī-nishīn*, or most commonly the "Dīwān," the shrine's religious leader was a direct lineal descendant of the saint and was believed to be Bābā Farīd's living representative. Both the Diwan and the shrine itself, a magnificent marble edifice constructed in the fourteenth century, are perceived to be carriers of Bābā Farīd's *baraka*, i.e., the spiritual power that enabled the saint to intercede with God on behalf of the devotees. Hence both the Diwan and the shrine functioned as intermediaries for an intermediary, as on-going vehicles of the saint's mediative power.

Underlying and reinforcing this conceptual world was an exchange of "religious goods" between the shrine's patrons and its clients—the chief patron being the Diwan, and the clients being the masses of *murīds*. For their part, the *murīds* made donations, usually cash contributions, that were called *naẕrāna*. As one cultivator from Lyallpur District put it, "We give *naẕrānas* to Dewan Sahib out of love, respect and regard for the Pir and to invoke his blessings for the good of the *murīd*."[3] In practical terms, this meant that *murīds* regularly made religious vows or "contracts" with Bābā Farīd, as a mediator between them and God, in hopes of receiving any number of concrete favors, such as female fertility, good crops, relief from illness, etc. Though the vow was made with the saint, the donations went to one of the saint's on-going representatives, namely, either the Diwan or the shrine as a whole. For this reason the manner in which *nazrāna* was given varied somewhat. Some *murīds* testified that, having made the pious visit to Pakpattan, they would "earmark" their *nazrāna* to go either in support of the shrine's public kitchen, or to the Diwan.[4] Others gave their *nazrāna* to the Diwan when he visited them in their villages. The amount of *nazrāna* varied, of course, with the means of the devotee.

If the *nazrāna* represented the flow of religious goods from the devotee inward to the shrine, the opposite flow, from the shrine outward to the devotees, took place in several ways. One of these was through the *langar*, or the public kitchen that the shrine housed and administered. Located in the shrine's courtyard just opposite Bābā Farīd's tomb, the *langar* was a vast operation, daily providing physical sustenance to the many pilgrims who came to pay respects and devotions at the shrine. One former worker in the kitchen estimated that between 240 and 320 lbs. (i.e. 3 or 4 *mans*) of wheat were consumed there every day, along with commensurate amounts of *dāl*, or split pea.[5]

Murīds also received religious goods of a more symbolic sort, consisting of sugar[6] or turbans, distributed only by the Diwan, and only on the occasion of particularly important shrine rituals at which he officiated. In part, the distribution of sugar represented the outward flow of Bābā Farīd's bounty and blessings. Symbollically, too, it linked both the Diwan and the *murīds* with their spiritual ancestor, Bābā Farīd, whose best-known epithet, Ganj-i Shakar, or "treasury of sugar," was associated with legends concerning the saint's severe austerities taken in pursuit of ascetic virtue.[7] The distribution of turbans—a powerful symbol of religious authority to be considered at greater length below—likewise served to connect *murīds* to the Diwan, and both of these parties to Bābā Farīd himself, whose spiritual authority at a very early period in the history of the shrine's cult came to be represented by his turban.[8]

The Shrine's Place in Time and Space

From the data recorded in the legal depositions, it does not appear that the *murīds* of the shrine saw any abrupt conceptual break between the life of Bābā Farīd, who died at the age of ninety in A.D. 1265, and the life of the shrine built over his grave. Indeed, many *murīds* referred to the saint and his shrine in the same terms, sometimes defining themselves as *murīds* of Bābā Farīd, and sometimes referring to themselves as *murīds* of the *gaddī*, or shrine. By conceptually fusing the saint and his shrine, *murīds* were able to understand the shrine as linking not only Heaven and Earth, but also past and present. The shrine *was* Bābā Farīd.

On the other hand, these same *murīds* had a very clear sense of their own tribal ancestors having, at some point in the historical past, been converted to Islam by Bābā Farīd. According to the depositions, this claim was made by many of the major endogamous clans that are spread throughout the southwestern Punjab, mainly as peasant agriculturalists. These clans, or *birādarīs* (brotherhoods), include the Wattu, the Sial, the Dogar, the Kathia, the Bhatti, and the Tiwana.[9] Typical of their statements is this by a fifty-four-year-old cultivator from Lyallpur District: "Our Tiwana tribe was converted by Baba Farid. Since then our relation of discipleship has been continued with the *gaddī*."[10] Similar is this statement by another Lyallpur farmer: "Baba Farid converted us Bhattis into Islam. Since that time we are the followers of the *gaddi* and respect the *gaddinashin* [i.e., *sajjāda-nishīn*, or Diwan] in office."[11] Now we know that most of those Jat or Rajput clans claiming conversion at the hand of Bābā Farīd were not in fact anywhere near the Pakpattan region in the thirteenth century when Bābā Farīd himself was living, meaning that in any literal sense such an event could not have occurred. But since, as is clear from these depositions, saint and shrine are conceptually fused in terms of religious function, no real contradiction exists. As the tribes were converted at some point in medieval history by the agency of the shrine, so also were they converted by Bābā Farīd.

As for conceptions of religious space, the *murīds* appear to have seen the shrine of Bābā Farīd as occupying one in a network of sacred *vilāyats*, or territories under the spiritual authority of one or another *pīr* (saint), which dot all of North India. Moreover, these shrines were perceived as related to each other in terms of a ranked hierarchy, with the shrine of Bābā Farīd being the supreme shrine of the Punjab, to which others were subordinate. The *sajjāda-nishīn* of one of these shrines listed the following as among the shrines subordinate to that of Bābā Farīd in Pakpattan: that of Shaikh Jamāl al-Dīn of Hansi, Hissar District, of Muḥammad Shāh in Basi Nau, Hoshiarpur District, of Niẓām al-Dīn Auliyā᾽ in Delhi, Piran Kaler in Saharanpur District, Golra Sharīf in Rawalpindi District, Taunsa Sharīf in Dera Ghazi Khan District, Mukhan Sharīf and Basal Sharīf in Campbellpore District, Uch Sharīf in Bahawalpur State, and the shrines of Kasur and Lakhneke in Lahore District, Kastiwala in Gurdaspur District, and Panipat in Karnal District.[12] Although one shrine located in the nearby town of Dipalpur had been given land by an earlier Diwan of Pakpattan and for this reason saw itself as subordinate to Bābā Farīd's shrine,[13] most of the "daughter" shrines of Bābā Farīd in the Punjab were founded by family descendants of Bābā Farīd, and hence they looked upon the shrine at Pakpattan as their spiritual superior. As we shall see below, this ranked hierarchy was ritually acted out according to an unwritten etiquette governing the attendance of shrine rituals by the *sajjāda-nishīns* of other shrines.

The spiritual potency, or *baraka*, of Bābā Farīd's shrine thus flowed out over the Punjab, infusing a series of subordinate shrines with sanctity. But the saint's *baraka* was seen as continuing to flow not only through the medium of such shrines, but also through living *pīrs* who likewise traced their spiritual, if not familial, descent from Bābā Farīd. Consider in this context how a fifty-four-year-old man from the neighboring town of Dipalpur, who was himself both a common cultivator and a *pīr*, identified himself: "I am a *ghulam* ["slave"] of Baba Farid's *silsila* ["spiritual order"]. I am a Watuzai Pathan and my ancestor of the 16th degree higher up was a disciple of Baba Farid. I am personally a *pir* of my tribe."[14] This *pīr*'s authority, in other words, stemmed from his descent not from Bābā Farīd's family, but from one of the saint's disciples. By this means Bābā Farīd's *spiritual* following spread out over many ethnically distinct groups, yet was sustained within such groups by living *pīrs* such as this gentleman, who served as a spiritual guide only for members of his own clan. Like the main shrine in Pakpattan, such *pīrs* also received cash payments from their *murīds*,[15] who readily identified the *pīrs* residing in or near their villages as their links with the shrine of Bābā Farīd in Pakpattan.[16] In fact, the very term "*pīr*" as used among the *murīds* in this court case could refer to a living saint related to Bābā Farīd, as well as to the shrine of the saint or of one of his descendants. Both *pīr* and shrine, after all, performed the same function—to sustain and transmit the blessings and intercessional power of Bābā Farīd.

The Shrine's Relationship to "This World"

Where did the devotees place the shrine's status in the political universe of the Punjab in the 1930s? In raising this issue we observe at the outset that this case was itself something of an anomaly from the standpoint of legal jurisdiction. Here was an Anglo-Indian civil court deciding, according to British legal procedures, a dispute between two Muslims over which one of them, according to Islamic Law as well as local custom, legitimately should succeed to the leadership of a Muslim shrine. In fact, religious considerations so permeated this dispute that one of the major points of contention that emerged was whether or not the former Diwan, Saʿīd Muḥammad, had received a dream in which Bābā Farīd revealed to him that his son Quṭb al-Dīn should succeed him as Diwan.

This situation implied two things, one respecting the proper jurisdiction of the Anglo-Indian legal system, and the other respecting the popular perception of the shrine's status in the political as well as religious world of the Punjab. As to the former, by being drawn into disputes such as was represented by this case, the Anglo-Indian courts were forced to make decisions that were strictly religious in nature: for example, that the former Diwan did in fact have a revelation from Bābā Farīd.[17] The case would seem, therefore, to have posed great theoretical difficulties for a ruling British government that professed to steer clear from interference with India's religious matters, illustrating some of the cultural implications of imperial rule.

More central to the purposes of this paper, the resolution of the shrine's internal conflicts in an Anglo-Indian court of law seemed to promote the popular perception of the shrine as a religious institution *only*, and to diminish perception of it as a political institution. Formerly, in the history of medieval Punjab, the Diwans of Pakpattan had frequently played important political roles, enjoying close relations with the sultans and Mughal emperors of Delhi. And during the decline of Mughal authority, the Diwans' political roles even outweighed their religious roles. As one important functionary of the shrine observed, from the early 1700s the Diwans of Pakpattan "were inclined to make conquests, to maintain armies, and to build forts. They themselves stopped giving spiritual education and employed Maulvīs, Imāms, Khaṭībs and Mubālighs for the purpose."[18] Lesser folk, *murīds* of the shrine, tended to see the Diwan's traditional function as both religious and political, and some *murīds* during the trial actually characterized the current Diwan as a *pīshwā*, or leader, "who leads us on the material and spiritual lines."[19]

But now that a non-Muslim foreign power was ruling India—a situation forcefully brought home by the very fact this dispute was being tried in an Anglo-Indian court—other *murīds* sensed a sharp separation between the Diwan's religious and political authority, with the Diwan and by implication the shrine being greatly reduced in point of political authority. One Jat *murīd* from Bahawalpur wistfully looked back upon the early days of Islam, when the first four caliphs combined political with religious authority, and contrasted that period with his own: "The *Khulafa-i Rashedin* who were four in number were both political and spiritual and religious heads. After *Khulafa-i Rashedin*, the *Khalifas* [caliphs] became the heads of [the] political department and the religious side became separate. On the political side, there is now no *Khalifa* in British India, only the British Government governs the country. The spiritual system was taken up by Baba Farid Shakar Ganj who was one of the various heads."[20] The fact that "only the British Government governs the country" had as its natural corollary, then, the enhancement of the shrine's *religious* status in the eyes of its devotees.[21]

The Shrine and Its Relationship to Formal Islam

What was, then, this religious status? One of the basic issues that emerged in the course of the litigation of this case—basic because it touched on the means of determining legitimate succession—was whether the shrine was to be understood fundamentally as a local institution which governed its affairs according to its own customs, or whether it was to be understood fundamentally as an Islamic institution, governing its affairs according to Islamic Law, the *sharīʿa*. The defendant, Quṭb al-Dīn, had been named Diwan by his father Saʿīd Muḥammad just before the latter died, and the defendant's lawyers vigorously argued that this kind of de facto primogeniture accorded with the shrine's traditional custom with respect to succession. It was logical, then, that because the *sharīʿa* is not generally interpreted as sanctioning primogeniture, the defendant's lawyers argued bluntly that "this *Gaddi* follows custom and not Mohammadan Law."[22] They also marshalled a wealth of historical evidence showing that previous Diwans had succeeded to the shrine's leadership as minors, though according to most interpretations the *sharīʿa* would not have sanctioned such succession.

On the other hand the plaintiff claimed to have been "elected" Diwan by the Chishti *birādarī*, which is the brotherhood of family descendants of Bābā

Farīd, and supported his arguments with pious appeals to early Islamic precedent. "The *gaddi* in dispute is an Islamic *gaddi*," the plaintiff argued. "It is governed by Mohammadan Law and not by custom. We are bound by *Shariat*, ever since the time of Holy Prophet, Hazrit Mohammad. What has happened ever since the time of [the] Holy Prophet is this, that those who claim to succeed to the *gaddi*, the disciples and the other rightful persons collect together and select one of them, who is considered to be the fittest person. The present *gaddi* is governed by the same rule of succession, as was in vogue during the time of *Khulafa-i Rashedin.* We, the descendants of Baba Farid, claim to be the descendants directly from Hazrit Umar, the second Caliph."[23] The issue of the shrine's Islamic character thus proved to be central to the entire case. But in soliciting opinions from *sajjāda-nishīns* of other shrines on this question, the Court failed to find much agreement: some argued that Muslim shrines could not follow local custom when it violated Islamic Law,[24] others that Islamic Law recognizes the use of local custom,[25] and one of them adopted the view that the *sajjāda-nishīn* is an autocrat, essentially above both custom and the *sharīʿa.*[26] The Court's final ruling on this question was an interesting compromise which saw the shrine basically as a local institution governing its affairs by its own traditional custom, but that, conveniently, this traditional custom happened to coincide with the *sharīʿa* since "Muhammadan Law itself reserves [customary] usage as the primary rule for governing succession to a religious institution."[27] The Court went on to cite several texts on Islamic jurisprudence to show that the *sharīʿa* even allows a shrine's leader to name his own successor.[28]

The Court, in other words, had it both ways. It saw the shrine at once as a local institution that ruled by its own custom, and as a Muslim institution whose traditions conformed with Islamic Law. In retrospect, this formula would seem to have provided the Court with a practical means of settling the dispute: the shrine could continue using its own customary practices, which the Government would simply declare as conforming with Islamic Law. In 1938, with the forces of Islamic reform and Muslim separatism rising on all sides in British India, the government could hardly have taken the politically dangerous step of declaring that the most popular Islamic shrine in the western Punjab was not, after all, Islamic.

Moreover, the vast majority of the shrine's *murīds* seemed to see the issue in much the same way. "The *gaddi* in dispute is bound by custom," said one fifty-two-year-old villager: "The *gaddi* in dispute is [an]Islamic *gaddi*, but is governed by custom. The *gaddinashin* [Diwan] must be of his father's caste, the mother's caste is immaterial. A Dewan can appoint whether he receives a revelation or not. But a revelation is generally received."[29] Here again we see a view of the shrine that found no basic conflict between customary practice and Islamic Law. This view would seem to have allowed devotees to follow familiar religious practices without facing the disturbing thought that they were in any way violating the dictates of the *sharīʿa*. On the other hand many of the urban *ʿulamāʾ*, for whom the whole culture of shrines and saints smacked of idolatry, would have flatly rejected this position. But this was 1938, the very twilight of British India. And though the demand for Pakistan was becoming increasingly strident, the *ʿulamāʾ* were not yet in positions of effective power.[30]

The Shrine and Graded Hierarchies

The shrine's religious status must be viewed, however, not only from the perspective of its position *vis-à-vis* formal Islam. One of the primary religious roles of the shrine that emerges from the many depositions of its devotees is one of establishing and maintaining a graded, spiritual hierarchy descending from God through the Prophet Muḥammad and Bābā Farīd to the Diwan and from him to his *khalīfa*s (spiritual adepts) and *murīd*s (spiritual affiliates). One also detects a perceived flow of grace, or *baraka*, from God to the *murīd* in which process the shrine is critical since it represents the visible, tangible point at which this grace is localized. It is in Pakpattan, a town that lay within easy reach of only several days' travel in the Punjab, that God's grace was made concrete and accessible, that Heaven and Earth met. It remains, then, to examine how each component of this spiritual hierarchy was perceived by the devotees themselves.

Although the *murīd*s seldom mentioned the Prophet Muḥammad in their depositions, he seems to have been visualized through the prism of the Islamic mystical tradition. One fifty-seven-year-old villager stated that Islam consisted of four principles—*ṭarīqat*, *sharīʿat*, *ḥaqīqat and maʿrifat*—and that it was the Prophet Muḥammad who had laid them down, using the following words: "*Shariat* is my word, *Tariqat* is my actions, *Haqiqat* is my conditions, and *Maʿrifat* is my mystery."[31] Ironically, though Muḥammad the Prophet was here cast generally in a Sufi light, Bābā Farīd the historical Sufi was cast as an infallable revealer of God's essence and a commander of God's Law. "I believe in the sanctity of the sayings, commands, or revelations of Baba Farīd," said a forty-year-old landholder from Ferozepore District; "Baba Farid's command can never be incorrect. As the *Sajjada Nashin* in office is a representative of Baba Farid, the same sanctity and reverence is shown to the *Gaddi Nashin* as is shown to Baba Farid."[32]

The above quotation and others previously cited illustrate decisively that the Diwan was seen above all as Bābā Farīd's living representative. Some *murīd*s, such as the one quoted above in note number twenty, seem to have viewed him as a sort of local caliph of Islam, though one lacking political authority since the British ruled the land. One witness even referred to the first four successors to the Prophet Muhammad as "*gaddī-nishīn*s" and not as caliphs,[33] a perception suggesting the extent to which the religious culture of the shrine permeated a *murīd*'s general outlook on Islam and on Islamic history.

As for how the *murīd*s viewed themselves in relation to the sociology of the shrine, they seem generally to have understood their inferior rank in the institution's hierarchy. When, for example, a fifty-five-year-old Jat peasant was asked why he did not sign a petition witnessing the installation of the plaintiff as Diwan, he replied, "Prominent persons were made to sign, and we smaller people were not asked to sign."[34] Moreover, the *murīds* almost without exception identified themselves not as individuals but in terms of a collective group, be that their kin group (*barādarī*) or the collective mass of *murīds*. Reflecting such kin-group identity, one villager belonging to the Wattu clan explained, "Khewa, one of my ancestors, was converted into Islam by Baba Farid, and since that time we have been following the *gaddi* in dispute."[35] Another *murīd* simply used as his reference point "we Jat people."[36] The other variety of collective identity transcended the kin group and tended to view all rural Muslims as devotees of Bābā Farīd. "All the Mohammadans are the *Murids* of Baba Farid," stated one villager, "and so is my family."[37]

At the bottom of the shrine's social hierarchy, then, were the peasant *murīds*, "we smaller people," belonging for the most part to Jat agricultural clans in southwestern Punjab. At the top, of course, was the Diwan, the supreme patron of all ritual functions at the shrine and the chief dispenser of Bābā Farīd's blessings. In between these was an endogamous clan of family descendants of Bābā Farīd, the Chishti clan (named after the Sufi brotherhood to which the saint had belonged), which possessed both economic privileges and ritual status *vis-à-vis* the local clans defining themselves as *murīds* of the shrine. An 1897 British Assessment Report for the Pakpattan region described the Chishtis as a "semi-religious Mussalman tribe" having "considerable local influence" and who "are not working agriculturalists, but depend for cultivation entirely on tenants."[38] As these tenants were drawn from among Jat clans whose members were *murīds* of the shrine, what we see here is a system embracing two tiers of lineages: an upper tier comprising the Chishti clan, and a lower tier comprising a number of subordinate lineages linked religiously to the shrine as *murīds*, and economically to the Chishti clan as tenant farmers.[39]

The Chishti clan was thus socially quite distinct from non-Chishti clans whose members were devotees of the shrine. In fact, the essential purpose of the trial of 1935-38 was to judge the plaintiff's claim that the prerogative to select a new Diwan belonged to the Chishti clan and not to the previous Diwan. Neither side in this case argued that the *murīds* should have had any say in the matter, and in fact the evidence shows that the *murīds* were clearly outside the decision-making process. As one villager testified, "the [Chishti] *biradri* was at first consulted about the appointment of the plaintiff. The *murids* were never consulted, they only said *Amin* to the *biradri's* election."[40] Even though the plaintiff lost this case, it is clear that the Chishti brotherhood—or certainly a substantial portion of it—claimed the status of the shrine's governing elite, and that many *murīds* acquiesced in this claim.

The claimed superior status of the Chishti clan was further enhanced by traditional marital practices that aimed at maintaining the clan's genealogical purity. So concerned with this issue was the Chishti clan that the leaders of a substantial faction of it—the faction supporting the plaintiff's cause—issued the following document on February 16, 1921:

> Be it noted by all people in general that the revered descendants of Hazrat Shah Ala-ud-Din Mauj Darja ... grandson of Hazrat Baba Sahib ... are the most honourable and distinguished of all the descendants of Farid (be he blessed), and have been contracting matrimonial relations among themselves, and that though they took girls of other families in marriage, yet they did not give away their daughters in marriage in other families for the last five or six centuries.... Whoever of the descendants of Mauj Darya gives his daughter in marriage in another family, should be excommunicated from the brotherhood, and it is also improper to maintain connections of any sort with him.[41]

It is well known that a rigid control over marital contracts, especially with respect to bride-giving, is a key mechanism by which the Hindu social order maintains its system of endogamous castes ranked in a graded hierarchy. The influence of Hindu social concepts on the functioning of the Chishti clan's social relations is therefore as remarkable as it is obvious. What is even more remarkable about this policy statement was that it appealed to Islamic Law for its justification. Although "all the descendants of Farid (be he blessed) are undoubtedly equal in lineal nobility," the document continued, "there are many traditions from the holy Prophet (peace be on him) in regard to prohibition from abandonment of one's own family in matters of matrimonial relations."[42]

In sum, it is evident from the documents of the Court's proceedings that the shrine had the objective function of establishing and maintaining not only a spiritual hierarchy, but also a social hierarchy as between the Diwan and his innermost family, the Chishti clan, and the many agricultural clans who as *murīd*s constituted the shrine's lay affiliates and traditional supporters. But these hierarchies were maintained not just by the fact of birth-ascribed kin groups or the marital policies of elite groups at the shrine. A series of elaborate initiatory and commemorative rituals had the effect of reinforcing existing hierarchal arrangements, while at the same time providing expressive meaning and cognitive order in the religious world of the shrine's devotees.

Rituals and Symbols at the Shrine

> Question: "What is the aim and object of the *Dastar bandi* performed on the fortieth day?"
> Answer: "So that all may come to know that such and such person has succeeded."[43]

The above extract hints at what is perhaps the most important on-going business of the shrine, namely, the projection of a dramatized image of the sacred order into this world. In Clifford Geertz's terms, the shrine provided its client clans of *murīd*s with a tiny "theater-state" of its own.[44] Through the ceremonies and celebrations that marked its liturgical calendar, it displayed the pageantry, order and beauty of the Court of God, albeit on a microcosmic scale. To the extent that religion itself can be understood as systems of symbols by means of which societies apprehend and comprehend the sacred order, Bābā Farīd's shrine provides the very stuff of religion.

The most common ritual that took place at the shrine was the initiation rite by which ordinary folk were formally made spiritual devotees of the shrine. Belonging to a kin group that at some distant point in time had been converted to Islam by Bābā Farīd did not automatically make one a *murīd* of the shrine.

One still had to participate in a formal initiation ceremony during which one made a solemn oath, known as *baiʿat*, swearing spiritual allegiance to Bābā Farīd and his spiritual descendants, including of course the incumbent Diwan. One devotee said that this ceremony properly occurred but once in one's lifetime,[45] and other testimony suggests that *murīd*s generally were young when initiated. Of those about whom we have information, one was age twenty-eight, one eighteen, one fourteen or fifteen, one ten or twelve, and one said simply that he was a young child when he took *baiʿat.*[46] The *baiʿat* ceremony itself was described in the following words: "I was made [a] disciple some 18 years back. I was made to go through the following ceremonies:—my hand was placed in the hand of the *Gaddi Nashin.* I offered *Nazrana*, and I was given spiritual instructions to lead a truthful and noble life. I was also given a 'Wazifa' for my recitation."[47] In this context the term *waẓīfa* referred to a prescribed liturgical formula, often a verse from the Qurʾān, which *pīrs* customarily gave their *murīd*s to recite in order to aid them in spiritual concentration. Three other *murīd*s reported having their forelocks (*lat*) clipped by the Diwan as part of their *baiʿat* ceremony.[48] This practice follows a basic Indian paradigm of religious initiation in which such clipping symbolizes for the initiate an avowal of an ascetic way of life. Since *murīd*s did not literally adopt ascetic vows when becoming devotees of the shrine of Bābā Farīd, the cutting of their forelocks must either be a remnant from earlier times when the *baiʿat* compact actually did involve such vows (Bābā Farīd himself was a renowned ascetic), or, as is more likely the case, it was borrowed from Hindu-Buddhist initiatory practices which, ancient as well as modern, associate the cutting of hair with the adoption of ascetic vows.

The *dastār-bandī*, or "turban-tying" ceremony, was one of the great religious dramas that took place at the shrine, since it was the ceremony by which a new Diwan was formally installed in office. Its purpose, as indicated in the quoted extract introducing this section, was to give public notice of the fact that Bābā Farīd had a new successor as his representative, a new spiritual custodian of his shrine. In many ways the ceremony mirrored the *baiʿat* ceremony for *murīd*s, since it too was concerned essentially with initiation, though of course on a far grander scale. For example, if in a *baiʿat* ceremony the *murīd*s forelocks were clipped, in the *dastār-bandī* ceremony the candidate's whole head was shaved.[49] The timing of the ceremony—the fortieth day after the death of the previous Diwan—coincided with the *ćhehlum*, which is a traditional day of mourning a person's death in Islam, thereby balancing the grief over the loss of a departed Diwan with the joy over the installation of a new one.

In the foreground of the *dastār-bandī* ceremony—or on the "stage," to follow the metaphor of the theater—were the most august figures associated with the shrine: the family of the Diwan, the most respected members of the Chishti clan, resident mystics living at the shrine, and *sajjāda-nishīn*s of all of Bābā Farīd's "daughter" shrines in the Punjab. The central ritual of the *dastār-bandī* ceremony at Bābā Farīd's shrine, as in others, was the placing of a special turban on the head of the new successor, symbolizing the legitimate succession of the saint's representative in the present time. Only somebody of equal or higher spiritual rank than the new *sajjāda-nishīn* could perform this ceremony, just as only a *pīr*, or someone of a spiritual rank higher than that of a *murīd* could perform a *baiᶜat* ceremony. But since there was no one within the shrine's own hierarchy possessing a higher rank than that of the Diwan-elect, this ceremony was normally performed by the head of an outside shrine having at least equal if not more spiritual authority than the one sponsoring the ceremony. In this way, while the heads of subordinate shrines attended a *dastār-bandī* ceremony as honored guests, only a head of a superior shrine actually performed it. Accordingly, on Februari 1, 1935, the eleven-year-old Quṭb al-Dīn, son of the recently deceased former Diwan, had the turban of succession placed on his head by the *sajjāda-nishīn* of the preeminent Chishti shrine of British India, that of Ḥaẓrat Muᶜīn al-Dīn Chishtī in Ajmer, Rajasthan.[50] True, Bābā Farīd's is the preeminent shrine of the Punjab. But the Ajmer shrine is the most eminent of all Chishti shrines in India since its patron saint, Muᶜīn al-Dīn Chishtī (d. 1236), founded the Chishti order of Sufis in India, and was the *pīr* of Bābā Farīd's own *pīr.* At one level, then, the *dastār-bandī* ceremony provided an opportunity for inter-shrine hierarchies to be acted out and confirmed.

In the background of the *dastār-bandī* ceremony, forming as it were the off-stage audience, throngs of *murīd*s assembled in the shrine's spacious courtyard in front of Bābā Farīd's tomb where the ceremony was performed. But it was not just for the Jat villagers, *murīd*s of the shrine, that the pageantry was performed. Hindu civic leaders and wealthy merchants also attended, and even participated. Accordingly, Ganpat Rai, a businessman and representative of a large market in Pakpattan, testified that "on the *dastarbandi* of the defendant *nazranas* were paid by us on behalf of the *Mandi* [market]."[51] In the same way, a certain Devi Bakhsh, a member of the Khatri caste, attended the ceremony and offered the new Diwan a turban and twenty-one rupees cash.[52] And Ram Rakha Mal, another Khatri and a member of Pakpattan's District Board, attended the ceremony, offering a turban and eleven rupees.[53] As Hindus, these gentlemen were probably not offering *naẕrāna* out of expectations consonant with the Muslim-oriented conceptual structure of the shrine, but out of respect for a local institution of great repute, and perhaps also out of a sense of civic responsibility. As one Hindu remarked, "there was a large number of persons including *Zamindar*s [landholders], the gentry, and the *sajjadanashin*s present."[54] Nonetheless, the presence of Hindus participating in this event suggests how, in the past, generations of people of various castes and creeds had become integrated into the outer, pageantry-oriented aspects of the shrine's activities.[55]

While the *dastār-bandī* ceremony properly occurred only when a new Diwan was installed, the anniversary of Bābā Farīd's death was celebrated in a vast pageant known in 1938 as the Bihishti *melā.* At other Indo-Muslim shrines, the anniversaries of the deaths of great saints are similarly celebrated, and done with a joyous air that would befit a wedding ceremony. This is no coincidence, of course, since this event is called the *ʿurs* celebration, which literally means "marriage with God." As such, it commemorates not the saint's death so much as his everlasting union with God, and hence his spiritual survival for purposes of passing on his grace, or *baraka*, to his devotees. But in the Bihishti *melā* the theme of salvation through loving devotion was made far more explicit than in most other Indo-Muslim shrines, since it was literally acted out by all participants. Called the *bihishtī darwāza*, or "Gate of Heaven," the south door of Bābā Farīd's tomb remained closed on all days of the year until the date of Bābā Farīd's *ʿurs*, the fifth of Muḥarram. On that day the Diwan personally unlocked and opened the gate, passed through it, and was then followed by throngs of *murīd*s estimated to number between fifty and sixty thousand.[56] All through the night and in states of intense religious ecstasy, the devotees filed through this "Gate of Heaven" and past Bābā Farīd's flower-bedecked tomb, thereby both commemorating and ritually reenacting the ascension of their patron saint to heaven. A description of this ceremony noted by a European visitor a century earlier, in 1833, vividly illustrates the salvation aspect of the ritual. When the gate is opened, the visitor observed,

> numbers of pilgrims, both Hindus and Mussalmans, come to visit the shrine, and all who pass through this doorway are considered saved from the fires of perdition. The door-way is about two feet wide, and cannot be passed without stopping, and the apartment itself is not capable of containing thirty people crowded together.... A superlative heaven is allotted to those who are first to enter the tomb on the day mentioned. The rush for precedence may, therefore, be better imagined than described. The crowd of pilgrims is said to be immense, and as they egress from the sacred door-way, after having rubbed their foreheads on the foot of the saint's grave, the air resounds with their shouts of Farid! Farid![57]

It is worth noting that because only the Diwan opened the gate, it was only through his agency that devotees gained access to Bābā Farīd, and only through the saint's agency that they gained access to Heaven. More than that, it seems that in the minds of the *murīd*s, a fixed order of precedence existed with respect to entering the "Gate of Heaven," despite the rush mentioned by the European visitor in 1833. "Dewan Sahib first opens the Bahishti Gate," explained a certain Khan Muḥammad in his deposition of August, 1938; "he enters the gate and thereafter his companions pass through that gate. The companions number about 100-125. After that, the pass-holders pass through it, they are about 400-500; after that, the *darveshes* of the *Hujra* [i.e., resident mystics], who number 1,000-1,200. After them the plaintiff, Ghulam Rasul and his party, pass through the Bahishti Gate, after that the *sajjadanashin*s of other institutions pass, and so on."[58] The great masses of common devotees, included among the "and so on" in the above quote, were allowed to enter through the gate only after the other dignataries had done so. The Gate of Heaven, after all, is a narrow one, and can be entered only one by one, in single file. All this suggests that the Bihishti ceremony served ritually to act out and confirm the sense of spiritual hierarchy that pervades the whole ethos of the shrine.

We also see that certain core symbols pervaded the initiatory and commemorative rituals of the shrine. Some were associated with medieval Indian royalty and served to emphasize the Diwan's supreme religious and administrative position. Thus when the Diwan would visit the shrine of Bābā Farīd's son-in-law in Pakpattan, Badr al-Dīn Isḥāq, on the occasion of that shrine's *ᶜurs* ceremony, the Diwan was carried on a palanquin (*palkī*). This means of conveyance, consisting of a litter borne on the shoulders of men by means of poles, was from ancient times traditionally reserved for persons of privileged status. One villager simply explained that on the occasion of Badr al-Dīn's *ᶜurs* "it is necessary for the *sajjadanashin* to go there in a *palki*."[59] Once there, moreover, gifts presented by the Diwan to Badr al-Dīn's descendant further suggested the style and magnanimity associated with Indo-Muslim nobles—100 rupees in cash, a horse, and a silver saddle.[60]

One symbol in particular, the turban, perhaps transcended all others in point of its repertoire and importance. Associated with traditional Sufi lore but also having ambiguous associations with the crown and thereby with royalty, the turban served as a vehicle both for religious legitimacy and for the distribution of Bābā Farīd's grace. As to the former, the depositions are full of evidence indicating that a proper successor to Bābā Farīd's shrine had to be "crowned" with a turban representing the saint's own turban, i.e., the *dastār-bandī* ceremony. Both disputants in this case accordingly went through such "turban-tying" ceremonies by way of laying claim to legitimate succession as Diwan. In the case of the defendant, who claimed that only a former Diwan could choose his successor, his own father, Diwan Saᶜīd Muḥammad, had placed a turban on the boy's head during the course of the Bihishti *melā* of 1933.[61] Later, on the occasion of the fortieth day after his father's death, the boy had a second *dastār-bandī* ceremony during which the *sajjāda-nishīn* of the Ajmer shrine placed the turban on the boy's head. As for the plaintiff, who claimed that a new Diwan must be elected by the Chishti clan, a special *dastār-bandī* ceremony was held at which representatives of the whole clan placed a turban on his head.[62]

It further appears that the turban used in the *dastār-bandī* ceremony, a special saffron-colored turban reserved only for the Diwan, was physically touched to the saint's tomb before being placed on the candidate's head.[63] This act decisively served ritually to link the new successor with Bābā Farīd himself, and rested in the popular belief that Bābā Farīd had used his own turban as a symbol of spiritual authority. One villager, for example, testified that the second Diwan, ᶜAlāᵓ al-Dīn Mauj Daryā (1281-1334), became Diwan by placing Bābā Farīd's very turban on his head when he was a child.[64] This seems to be a truncated version of a story given in more detail by another villager, to the effect that as a child, ᶜAlāᵓ al-Dīn had one day playfully put Bābā Farīd's turban on his head. When a servant objected, Bābā Farīd, then an old man, pardoned the child's behavior saying that the boy would one day be his successor anyway.[65] Still another witness testified that when the first Diwan died and a dispute arose over who should succeed him, the great saint of Delhi, Khwāja

Niẓām al-Dīn Auliyāʾ, came to Pakpattan to arbitrate. At his instance, the story continued, "the turbans of all the rival claimants were emersed in water. The turban of Dewan Alau-ud-Din Mauj-i Darya came out coloured, consequently, the *Bradari* accepted Dewan Alau-ud-Din Mauj-i Darya as the proper *Gaddi Nashin* to the exclusion of all other claimants."[66] In all of these versions we find the common assumption that the turban, used in the proper ritual context, was uniquely empowered to endow the wearer with Bābā Farīd's own spiritual authority.

A second use of the turban was as a carrier in distributing Bābā Farīd's grace among his devotees. As one sixty-year-old villager remarked, "*pecha*s [turbans] are distributed at the annual urs only by [the] *sajjadanshin* and nobody else. At that time, [the] *sajjadanashin* has hundreds of *pecha*s with him. He must distribute those *pecha*s personally."[67] Yet turbans were passed in the opposite direction, too. We have seen that oftentimes *naẕrāna* given to the Diwan by devotees, or simply by well-wishers, consisted of turbans in addition to cash. In this sense, we find the turban employed as a symbol of a shared cultural heritage. Since it got passed to and from persons otherwise occupying different positions in the social hierarchy, the *pecha* or "honorary" turban promoted egalitarian feelings of a shared, common tradition. On the other hand the word *dastār* referred to the turban which served to separate Bābā Farīd's legitimate successor from the common crowd, thereby having the opposite effect of maintaining hierarchy. Indeed, it is in the turban's rich symbolic repertoire that we see its capacity to express and sustain values so central to the shrine. Accordingly, in different contexts, the turban could even express values that might otherwise appear mutually antagonistic, i.e., hierarchy of religious status and commonality of cultural inheritance.

Court of God, Court of Man

To conclude, the shrine of Bābā Farīd in Pakpattan provides a striking example of how Islam, the religion par excellence "of the Book," has been in one instance mediated among common villagers most of whom were illiterate. For them it was the shrine, and less so the Book, which manifested the juncture "where the contrasted poles of Heaven and Earth met." Through its elaborate rituals, grand processions and colorful pageantry, the shrine displayed a sense of divine magnificence and divine mercy. It displayed, in short, the Court of God. Not that Bābā Farīd himself was confused with God. This would of course have been blasphemous idolatry, as was fully understood by one old cultivator who declared, "doing *sajda* [prostration] to the tomb of Baba Farid under Mohammadan Law is not permissible."[68] Rather, though the Court of God as a cosmological construct seemed to lie beyond the devotee's immediate grasp, he did have a "friend in court," as it were, who represented his interests there. This "friend in court," this special pleader, was Bābā Farīd.

In the years 1935 to 1938 this Court of God conception of the world was contrasted by a conception made manifest in the town of Montgomery, some

25 miles from the hallowed marble domes of Pakpattan, in the Court of the senior subjudge of the Montgomery District, British Punjab. In the Court of Man, the world is held together not by an unseen Presence, but by principles, called "laws," which are whatever men state them to be. In British India, the effect of such laws was to render state sanction to whatever local customs the courts judged were already being practiced by a majority of the people. Accordingly, in the Court of Man superhuman evidence such as a revelation from Bābā Farīd was inadmissible. As the District Court Judge commented in his final verdict, "Whatever weight an argument as to revelation may be entitled to in a purely religious or metaphysical discussion, it cannot, I think, prevail ... in a Court of law at the present day."[69]

The case examined here might therefore appear to have represented a clash of two conceptual systems. But did they really clash? As we have seen, the District Court in the end merely ratified what it deemed to be the customary practice with regard to succession at the shrine, and then declared its judgment to be in conformity with Islamic Law. To the masses of devotees in Pakpattan, however, the little drama unfolding in the district courthouse in Montgomery was apparently irrelevant to their religious concerns, their goals, and their concerns. "I am a follower of the *Gaddi Nashin* whosoever may be occupying it," stated one of Bābā Farīd's *murīds*.[70] Though they could choose whom they wanted as Diwan, this sentiment seems to suggest, the learned lawyers of Montgomery could not really effect the substance of what this shrine was all about. Thus in the last analysis, if this sentiment was typical, the Court of God quite transcended the Court of Man in the eyes of the shrine's common devotees.

NOTES

1 Peter Brown, *The Cult of the Saints: Its Rise and Function in Latin Christianity* (Chicago: University of Chicago Press, 1981), p. 3.

2 The past tense is used here and in the following discussion because the data on which the discussion is based belong to the period 1935-38. It is fair to assume, however, that the most general aspects of the shrine as described here hold as true for the present day as for the 1930s.

3 *Lahore High Court, Regular First Appeal No. 93 of 1939: Dewan Ghulam Rasul vs. Ghulam Qutab-ud-din*, 5 vols., (Lahore, 1940), vol. 2, p. 239.

4 *Ibid.*, vol. 1, p. 155; vol. 2, pp. 28, 239.

5 *Ibid.*, vol. 2, p. 256.

6 *Ibid.*, vol. 1, p. 133.

7 "By continuous fasting," noted a British gazetteer in 1884, "his body is said to have become so pure that whatever he put into his mouth to allay the cravings of hunger, even earth and stones, was immediately changed into sugar, whence his name Shakar-Ganj, or sugar store. Another version of the story is that the saint, when hungry, used to tie a wooden cake (*chappati*) or a branch of wooden dates to his stomach, and that this composed his sole nourishment for thirty years. The truth of the story is vouched for by the preservation of the identical cakes and dates to this very day. They are kept "at his shrine...." *Punjab District Gazetteers. Montgomery District* (Lahore, 1884), p. 184.

8 The *Jawāhir-i Farīdī*, an important collection of the lives of Bābā Farīd's spiritual and lineal descendants completed in 1623, records that all the major rituals associated with the shrine,

including those dealing with Bābā Farīd's turban, had become instituted in the generation following the saint's death, that is, in the late thirteenth century. See *Jawāhir-i Farīdī*, comp. ᶜAli Asghar Chishti (Lahore, 1883-84), pp. 298-300.

9 *Lahore High Court*, vol. 1, pp. 124, 138, 188, 225; vol. 2, pp. 80, 87.

10 *Ibid.*, vol. 2, p. 87.

11 *Ibid.*, vol. 2, p. 80.

12 *Ibid.*, vol. 1, p. 180.

13 *Ibid.*, vol. 2, p. 51.

14 *Ibid.*, vol. 2, p. 13.

15 *Ibid.*, vol. 2, p. 164.

16 *Ibid.*, vol. 1, p. 193.

17 In his final judgment, delivered on December 2, 1938, Judge Guru Datta ruled, *inter alia*: "I decide that the defendant has sufficiently succeeded in proving that Diwan Said Muhammad had received revelation and that the defendant's nomination was made on the strength of that." *Ibid.*, vol. 3, p. 290.

18 *Ibid.*, vol. 2, p. 278.

19 *Ibid.*, vol. 2, pp. 240-41.

20 *Ibid.*, vol. 2, p. 288.

21 For a perception discussion of the intrusion of British power in Punjabi shrines and the implications this had for the modes of shrine leadership, see David Gilmartin, "Shrines, Succession and Sources of Moral Authority," in a forthcoming volume edited by Barbara Metcalf on *Moral Conduct and Authority: The Place of Adab in South Asian Islam* (Berkeley and Los Angeles: University of California Press).

22 *Lahore High Court*, vol. 1, p. 12.

23 *Ibid.*, vol. 2, p. 93.

24 *Ibid.*, vol. 3, pp. 65, 121, 151, 212.

25 *Ibid.*, vol. 3, pp. 86, 97.

26 "It depends on the sweet will of the *sajjada nashin*," argued the *sajjāda-nishīn* of the shrine of Jamāl al-Dīn Hansawī, "He can do about the shrine whatever he pleases." *Ibid.*, vol. 3, p. 140.

27 *Ibid.*, vol. 3, p. 254.

28 *Ibid.*

29 *Ibid.*, vol. 2, p. 138.

30 For a discussion of how the Government of Pakistan has dealt with the culture of shrines and saints since 1947, see Kathy Ewing, "Sufism, Cosmology and the Pakistani Government," paper presented at the 77th annual meeting of the American Anthropological Association, November, 1978.

31 *Lahore High Court*, vol. 2, p. 43.

32 *Ibid.*, vol. 1, p. 220.

33 *Ibid.*, vol. 1, 150.

34 *Ibid.*, vol. 1, p. 148.

35 *Ibid.*, vol. 2, p. 64.

36 *Ibid.*, vol. 2, p. 31

37 *Ibid.*, vol. 1, p. 205.

38 P. J. Fagan, *Assessment Report for Pakpattan Tahsil, Montgomery District*, 1897 (Lahore, 1898), p. 50.

39 Away from the immediate area around Pakpattan, this connection was probably religious only, and not economic, since the dominant Chishti clan, many of whose members were landholders, were traditionally clustered around the town of Pakpattan.

40 *Lahore High Court*, vol. 2, pp. 18-19.

41 *Ibid.*, vol. 4, p. 27.

42 *Ibid.* The fact that the former Diwan had given his own daughter in marriage outside the lineage constituted, as the judge shrewdly observed in his final judgment, one of the ultimate causes of the entire dispute, since that act had touched off the profound discord within the Chishti *barādarī* that erupted only after the former Diwan died in 1934. See *Ibid.*, vol. 3, p. 298.

43 *Ibid.*, vol. 3, p. 110.
44 Clifford Geertz, *Islam Observed: Religious Development in Morocco and Indonesia* (Chicago: University of Chicago Press, 1971), p. 38. "See also his *Negara: the Theater State in Nineteenth-Century Bali* (Princeton University Press, 1980), especially chapter four."
45 *Lahore High Court*, vol. 2, p. 39.
46 *Ibid.*, vol. 1, pp. 109, 199, 160, 222, 186.
47 *Ibid.*, vol. 1, p. 109.
48 *Ibid.*, vol. 1, pp. 160, 162.
49 *Ibid.*, vol. 1, p. 170.
50 *Ibid.*, vol. 3, p. 215; vol. 2, p. 163.
51 *Ibid.*, vol. 2, p. 174.
52 *Ibid.*, vol. 2, p. 224.
53 *Ibid.*, vol. 2, p. 223.
54 *Ibid.*
55 This integrative aspect of the shrine constitutes one of its oldest and historically most significant roles. See my article, "The Political and Religious Authority of the Shrine of Baba Farid in Pakpattan, Punjab," in a forthcoming volume on moral authority in Indo-Muslim civilization edited by Barbara Metcalf (see note 21 above).
56 *Punjab District Gazetteers. Montgomery District* (Lahore, 1884), p. 185.
57 Lieut. F. Mackeson, "Journal of Captain C. M. Wade's Voyage from Lodiana to Mithankot by the River Satlaj on His Mission to Lahor and Bahawalpur in 1832-33," *Journal of the Asiatic Society of Bengal* 6 (1837): 192.
58 *Lahore High Court*, vol. 2, p. 249.
59 *Ibid.*, vol. 2, p. 153.
60 *Ibid.*
61 *Ibid.*, vol. 2, pp. 181, 193.
62 *Ibid.*, vol. 1, p. 47.
63 *Ibid.*, vol. 2, pp. 55, 169, 181. Since the plaintiff was not given access to the shrine for his *dastār-bandī* ceremony, this aspect of the rite had to be omitted in his case.
64 *Ibid.*, vol. 1, p. 170.
65 *Ibid.*, vol. 1, pp. 102-103. The same witness added that Bābā Farīd also placed saliva from his own mouth into that of the boy "in order to impart spiritual light from himself to the boy." See *Ibid.*, vol. 1, p. 103.
66 *Ibid.*, vol. 1, p. 158.
67 *Ibid.*, vol. 2, p. 104.
68 *Ibid.*, vol. 2, p. 39.
69 *Ibid.*, vol. 3, p. 289. Nonetheless, it is a measure of the genius of human institutions that on the very next page, this same judge made a ruling on the fact of Bābā Farīd's revelation. See above, footnote 17.
70 *Lahore High Court*, vol. 1, p. 138.

Contributions to Asian Studies, Vol. XVII

Islam and Custom in Nineteenth-Century India

The Reformist Standard of Maulānā Thāwanī's Bihistī Zewar

BARBARA DALY METCALF
University of Pennsylvenia, Philadelphia, Pe., U.S.A.

THIS PAPER is about an attempt that was made to persuade Muslims in "Hindustan" that their thinking and behavior violated the true order of things, that is to say, Islam as correctly understood.[1] In the late nineteenth century in north India, a group of men, scholarly and pious, set out to argue by any means of propaganda they could lay their hands on, that Islam as practiced in their society was misguided. To make matters worse, they felt, Muslims had come to think of themselves as faithful while the very practices they held to were in fact deviant. One part of the concern of this group was to eliminate what they called "custom" (*rasm*, pl. *rusūm*; *riwāj*; *dastūr*). They analyzed custom as observances and occasions socially practiced, those that involved family (*kunbā*) and the extended brotherhood (*birādarī*) of intermarrying relations. They also exposed certain objectionable individual practices—keeping dogs or sporting an unacceptable haircut—but their greatest criticism was directed toward ceremonies that marked life stages and the festivals of the calendrical year.

The criticisms leveled against custom were part of a larger program of teachings, all of which were directed to the persuasion of individual Muslims that they had to take charge of their own well-being and salvation by developing characteristics of discipline and self-control and by adhering to the specific injunctions of the scriptural sources of the faith, the Qurʾān and the *sunna* of the Prophet. Custom was seen to thwart adherence to scriptural injunctions; as such, no personal matters of concern regarding family or kin could be permitted to intervene. Nor could old habits of resorting to saintly intervention be tolerated. In addition to custom, the reformers decried those practices—ones I shall not treat of here—that centered on the shrines of the medieval Sufi saints, and that called on the believer to make offerings and attend ceremonies but did not require him or her to make an individual commitment to fulfill the Law or to cultivate one's own personal qualities. Links to the shrines or even kin relationship to holy and learned men was, in the reformers' view, simply not enough, as the following story reveals:

> Hazrat Halimah Saʿdiyya, may God be pleased with her, nursed our Messenger, God's peace and blessings upon him! Later she joined him at the time when he was waging war on the city of Ṭāʾif, bringing along her husband and son. He praised her greatly and spread

> out his shawl and sat her upon it.... Despite her deep bond [ʿ*ilāqa*] to the lord(s), she knew that without belief she would have no reward on the basis of connection alone. Thus it was that she came to him and accepted the faith. O Women! Never put your trust in being among the offspring of a holy man or the mother of a scholar or a son who has memorized the Qurʾān, assuming that one of them will effect your pardon. If you yourself are not religious, these people cannot talk to our dear God [*Allāh Miyāṅ*] on your behalf and nothing will come of your connection.[2]

The reformers were concerned with the individual's relation to God, not with relations to familial institutions or to religious intermediaries as they existed.

The tension between localized social enmeshment and individual participation in a universal religion is one familiar from the history of Christianity as well as from Islam and was, in neither case, solved once and for all at the origin of these religions. It recurs, rather, in different places and at different times, and to different degrees. The call on the part of the late nineteenth-century Hindustani reformers was not "to abandon all." The individual was still expected to fulfill the obligations of a hierarchic, patriarchal society in which the rich and the poor, the older and the younger, the male and the female each sustained obligations to each other and exchanged deference from the one in return for kindness from the other. The individual was, however, expected to shift energy and attention and wealth away from familialistic involvements and toward the observances and methods of personal development taught by the reformers and argued to be normative for all Muslims at all times.

In place of external actions of reciprocity to shrines, the reformers taught their followers to take a human guide (a person like the reformers themselves), who embodied the correct teachings of the faith. His personality and guidance were to be internalized, thus to become far more effective than any lifeless writings in a book. The beloved saints, and women like Hazrat Haliman Saʿadiyya mentioned above, were to be cherished not as mediators but as examplars, as, indeed was the Prophet himself. As the ultimate analogue of the other in these dyadic relationships stood, of course, Allah, here made proximate as Allāh Miyāṅ, "our dear God," as translated above. The epithet is striking, for *miyāṅ*, a Hindi term, is normally used for the husband or household head, or, as *miyāṅjī*, for the schoolteacher. Allah is given a human face as a respected elder whose loving will must be obeyed.

Concern with custom was thus part of some far-reaching changes in social relationships and psychological identity. There is no reason to think that the customs existed as "infiltrations" from Hinduism even if they shared the idiom of Hindus customs, nor that they were primordial urges nipping away at some higher form of truth. The reformers themselves may have had some such notions, but we do well to remember that their opponents were equally confident that much of what was opposed had equal sanction in Islam. The opponents to reform saw it as nothing less than lack of respect for religiously ordained social relationships and, more serious yet, lack of respect for the beloved saints and even the Prophet of God.

We, however, are more likely to find a movement like that of the reformers plausible. This, it has been argued, is so because of persistent European eighteenth-century notions that man is not a natural monotheist but in his unenlightened state is given, through fear and anxiety, to notions of the divine which are personalistic and polytheistic.[3] The resultant "two-tiered model" of religious life would in this case imply that the capitulation of true Islam to superstitions of the vulgar was now being turned back. Such a theory assumes that ideas, like germs, exist in a socio-economic vaccum, with the "lower tier" a particularly virulent strain. Instead of this, we can see the custom-laden religion as having an affinity to a more locally-organized society, and the reform religion, as more apposite to the increasingly integrated social and political world of its times; a world, moreover, in which no Muslim stood at the apex of intermediary organizations. The customs were, in fact, in no sense associated with the humble or with mere villages: it was the rich and influential with the means to carry out ceremonial displays who were particular targets of reform. To call customary religion "popular religion" would therefore be misleading. The reformers themselves did not identify objectionable customs as Hindu, except incidentally, nor as the preserve of lower class or ordinary people. They knew that the the changes they espoused touched the whole range of Muslim society.

What the reformers did do, and, once the issue was joined, their opponents did as well, was to insist on a reconsideration of the meaning of the scriptural sources of the faith. This kind of attention to scripture in not a constant in Islam even if scripture as symbol is unquestioned. The Law (*sharīᶜat*) can exist as symbol, not necessarily as detailed and requisite code. But once reformers turned to the sources, the opponents could only answer in kind. Moreover, once the core of normative teachings was revivified—the requisite worship (*ᶜibādāt*); the regulations of personal status; the tenets of *tauḥīd*, prophecy, and the miracle of the Qurʾān; and the beliefs (*agāʾid*)—they too could only be generated with greater vigor.[4] But the exact teachings and the exact prohibitions could vary. Since the idiom of the debate was legal, the issues often turned on principles of jurisprudence. The very customary practices condemned by one side could be santioned by a principle like jurisprudential eclecticism (the use of more than one of the four legitimate Sunni law schools within the same proceeding) or by an extension of the category of what was a "strong" *ḥadīth* conveying the *sunna* of the Prophet. The efforts of the reformers must be seen as an attempt to spread normative Islam, but only in the sense that attention to the sources is itself normative, and a limited cluster of normative elements—albeit with some differences in interpretation—was given increased attention.

The Context of the Bihishtī Zewar

Reconsideration of the scriptural sources of the faith has become a major feature of Islam in the modern world. The Muslims of British India were among those who, in particular, made sustained and varied attempts to define what it meant to be Muslim. They examined their own culture and distinguished over and over, in a wide variety of contexts, what was legitimate and what was not. One particularly important group of those engaged in this enterprise were religious scholars associated with an influential movement of intellectual reformulation, social reform, and education that was known as the Deobandi movement after the town, Deoband, some ninety miles northeast of Delhi, which was the site of a theological seminary founded in 1867.[5] The stimulus to their efforts was the end of Muslim rule and all the disjunctures—social, economic, and political—that that change entailed. The form their efforts took was shaped by the imposition of British rule, for the imperial presence prevented any movement with military or messianic claims. At the same time it provided Muslims with institutional models and technological means for education and propaganda that gave them an inconspicuous but effective program for change. Those who participated in this movement found in it a source of community and self-esteem, for the movement insisted on the worth of pristine Islam while recognizing the failure of its contemporary exponents. Their reformed Islam would, they believed, make Muslims great in a material and worldly sense once again. Meanwhile it gave each individual certain guidelines and attitudes to shape and give meaning to his or her life, nurtured by relationships to exemplars, seen and unseen.

No British were involved in the movement nor did its participants use English in their work. Yet many aspects of their teachings strike one as having an affinity to modern patterns of social and economic integration and to the personal requirements of bureaucratic organizations and even, possibly, a capitalist economy. As noted above, the movement eschewed extravagant customary practices, including lavish weddings and dowries; and downplayed local saintly cults in favor of individual responsibility to scripturalist norms. Its participants were to be guided by a high degree of internal discipline and a willingness to forego immediate material pleasures. It denied the importance of carefully graded social ranking in favor of a broad definition of respectability, based in part on shared religious style, as a basis for marriage and other social relations. These changed teachings, moreover, fostered a higher degree of cultural distinction from the non-Muslims who shared with them Indian territory, although, again, this was not a self-conscious goal.

Indeed it is striking how little these historical processes of change appear in the language of the reformers. They did not see themselves as modernizing or creating a separate polity. They were involved in teaching Muslims to be good Muslims and believed themselves to be in the company of great reformers of the past, including the Prophet himself, for whom precisely the ending of false custom and the creation of religiously responsible individuals had been central. They were engaged in renewal (*tajdīd*) of the teachings of the Qurʾān and the Prophet.

This concern is evident in one of the most influential of the Deobandi books, the *Bihishtī Zewar* of Maulānā Ashraf ʿAlī Thānawī. Written for Muslim women at the turn of the century, it is an encyclopedic work of over one thousand pages including detailed discussions of the religious law; not only ritual law, but family, commercial and financial law. It includes sections on household management, the principles of Islamic medicine, biographies of good women, personal development, and the section discussed here, "A Statement on Customs." The book is widely available even today, and it has been translated into many other languages beyond the Urdu in which it was originally written.

The very existence of the book is telling. It represents the new, inexpensive publication permitted by the technology of the late nineteenth century and exploited by pedagogues of a wide variety. More specifically, it exemplifies the reformers' effort to carry their teachings to hitherto uninformed groups among Muslims, here women specifically. Reformist teachings and writings in this case penetrated to an arena that had been left to older women who instructed the younger by example and advice. The reformers were concerned to intrude on matters of life-stage ceremonies and calendrical rituals precisely because they were so much in the hands of women. They felt constrained to intervene the more since women were the target of alternate advice in similar form through missionary publications directed at them.

Custom and Thānawī's Opposition

The subject of custom is a significant one for Muslims. Muslims in all areas have been conscious of the extent to which their local culture has acquired certain practices that are not explicitly sanctioned in Islamic scripture. The distinction of what is custom is not always explicitly made and anything not evidently objectionable is typically incorporated as acceptable or even in some sense Muslim, that is as a defining feature of the community. The incorporation of custom is evident in the recognition that certain practices can be legitimated in Islamic law as *ʿurf* or *ʿāda*. Thus, rules governing inheritance in parts of India long followed customary rather than *sharīʿat* norms.

The argument made by the reformers against custom is not on the ground that all custom in itself is objectionable or that the origin of the custom is decisive. What one might call the "archaeology" of the custom is relatively unimportant. Thus, an outsider might distinguish some of the customs as Hindu in origin, some as common to certain kinds of familial structures, and some as evolving from Sufi practices. Occasionally some reference to origin is adduced and it is noted (by reference to *ḥadīth*) that one ought not resemble unbelievers. Generally, however, custom is scrutinized and measured against the teaching of scripture, not by its presumed origin. In this sense the argument of the *Bihishtī Zewar* draws upon a style of discourse that is characteristically Islamic, namely that of assessing acts in the light of scriptural standards.

The de-emphasis of origin in the chapter on custom is reflected in the division of the chapter into three subsections based on ascending degrees of popular approval. The first brief section (pp. 1-6) examines those customs which all Muslims are said to deem illegitimate but so trivial as to be tolerated. The second section, the longest (pp. 6-63), describes those customs wrongly considered to be legitimate. The final section (pp. 63-82) lists those practices Indian Muslims have considered not merely legitimate but even praiseworthy, practices worthy of reward (*sawāb*) and encompassed in religion (*dīn kī bāt*). The exercise of the author is to break through these perceptions, showing that the whole spectrum, from those customs known to be sinful to those taken as meritorious, are in fact matters of serious sin. The argument is simple and direct and in each case custom is shown to be explicitly sinful or to lead to some sin. Quotations from sacred authority are provided in a style accesible to anyone. None of the discussions of jurisprudential principles characteristic of reformist writings are directed to the *ʿulamāʾ* as such.

At times references to sacred authority are paired with references to reason (*ʿaql*). Man's reason does not, however, provide an autonomous authenticating source, as such a distinction might imply. Reason in fact here means reasoned discrimination of the law of God.[6] What one knows by reason one also knows by correct reading of the Law. What is rational or natural is in fact what is legal: a normal person hates sin just as he hates what goes against his or her nature (*ṭabīʿat*).[7] In this conception, to be natural is not to be unfettered but rather to be like the animals and plants and inanimate objects of nature, all of which follow the cycles and habits ordained for them. For humans, those cycles and habits are precisely the Law which they alone choose either to follow or to ignore.

In discussing feigned exchanges during ceremonies, Thānawī despairs of current behavior: "Alas, that the most rational, those who teach reason to others, even they are sunk in this unreasonable custom.... In truth custom [*riwāj*] is a strange thing, for no matter how much something is against reason, even the most rational are not ashamed to do it."[8] He can only conclude that a curtain has fallen over people's reason and that they are like children whose reason has not been developed and are misled by appearances into eating the sweets that make them sick. Given what seems to him the self-evident rationality of his teachings, Thānawī argues that following them will bring not only divine reward but a sense of right and well-being. To encourage the ending of delayed reciprocal exchanges (*neʾotā*), he writes, "In this besides the pleasure of God and the Messenger(s), how great comfort and satisfaction there is!";[9] and on custom in general, perhaps wishfully, he notes, "Everyone is distracted and constrained on account of these customs; everyone thinks that if these customs had not existed, it would be better."[10]

Implicit in Thānawī's argument is the notion that custom thwarts the natural order among humans and between humans and God. Adherence to custom has become an inappropriate source of status, false grounds for winning approval in society. Custom not only makes adults act like children but encourages the powerful to mistreat the weak, and thus to violate the order that ought to exist between masters and servants. The woman after childbirth, for example, is considered as an untouchable (*najas*, *ćhūt*) and the husband, whose child it is, is not permitted near her.[11] Other customs explicitly reverse the proper roles of the sexes. Thus during dancing and revelry, women wear men's hats or dress like men, which is forbidden.[12] After the marriage the husband declares to the wife, "I am your slave" or "You are the lion and I am the sheep" thus reversing the proper relation between the superior husband and his obedient wife.[13] Customs also distort the proper place of Muslims in relation to non-believers, both by emulating their practices and by such rules as those requiring gifts to untouchable *bhangīs* instead of to Muslim poor.[14]

A certain humaneness breaks through Thānawī's outrage at these deviations. He is appalled at the unfairness of the treatment of servants, writing of the palanquin bearer: "Everyone knows that no wages are fixed for the *kahār*, nor is any consideration given to whether he works willingly or under constraint. These people have problems, too. They may be sick or their wives and children may be sick—but people send them off with a good shoe-beating.... Most of the time these people are forced to work. This is tyranny (a violation of order) and sin...."[15] Similarly the objections to the customs of marriage are reinforced by what Thānawī judges to be inhumane treatement of a young girl: "Just think, until now she used to wander here and there over the whole house. Now, suddenly, she is forced to sit in a corner.... These are all your own devisings and absurdities."[16] And of her similar treatment at the groom's house he judges her a prisoner: "God knows what crime this poor creature has committed to be put in solitary confinement!"

Custom subverts not only the natural order of worldly relationships but relationships that extend from this world to the other. The *Fātiḥa* observance [the assignment of religious merit for some good work] for the dead, for example, is judged to accord power to the dead in opposition to the belief that all power derives from God alone. Elaborate marriage customs imply that the participants consider themselves greater than the Prophet and his Companions who acted with simplicity. To deny widow remarriage, a prevalent restriction, is to set oneself above the Prophet himself, all of whose wives but one were widows.

Since Thānawī knows and teaches the single system humans ought to accept, he does not present custom as part of a structured alternate pattern of relationships and values that one would weigh as a whole against his Islamic pattern. He notes from time to time that a particular custom has a meaning for Hindus but he never discusses the interrelationships of customs as part of a systematic whole. As discussed below, many of the customs he describes appear to be part of three of the social institutions of this area: *ne'otā*, the system of delayed reciprocity; *bhāt*, the practice of gifts to daughters and sisters; and *jajmānī*, the hierarchic patronage relationships of material, ritual and service exchange. Thānawī, however, is concerned only to weigh each custom discretely and judge each to be a violation of Islamic norms.

To show the vacuity of customary practices Thānawī employs the rhetorical device of discussing them, ironically, in the language of the Law

which they in fact destroy. When cast in those terms, the distance between foolishness and truth is presumably the more apparent. Custom forms its own *sharīʿat*, Thānawī writes, using the Hindi term, a *man Ghaṛat* (self-devised) *sharīʿat* which is at once a linguistic anomaly and the opposite of what is taken to be the only legitimate source of authority, namely revelation from all time and for all time.[17] Customary gifts and dues are consistently referred to as being a *farẓ-i wājib*, a necessary obligation. Practices are often described as being considered more important and more a source of pride than the rituals of the faith. Thānawī writes ironically about the share given to the singing woman and to the barberess: "The fortieth share due our dear God [*Allāh Miyāṅ*] is not such a duty. The tenth share of the field is not so obligatory."[18] In a similar reversal, in discussing the practice of girls burying their faces in their hands during the custom of "showing the face," he writes: "This is such a duty that if she does not do it she is known as shameless, immodest and lacking pride throughout the whole brotherhood. Everyone acts as shocked as if a Muslim had turned infidel!"[19] "[Rice pudding placed in the bride's hand is more important than] if never in her life she [would] have the grace of the canonical prayer."[20]
On sending a barber to arrange an engagement instead of simply writing a letter, Maulānā Thānawī says, "To consider a matter not fixed as necessary in the Law as more necessary than something that is ...—is that to oppose the Law or not?"[21] One has created an alternate law and reversed all categories. "On this day, all sins and immodesty become *ḥalāl* (legally permitted.)"[22]

The misconstrual of these customs is driven home in one of Thānawī's particularly striking passages when he discusses the custom of keeping the new bride immobile in her husband's home. Only if someone happens to make arrangements for her does she read the canonical prayer. Mocking this as the practice of an alternate school of law, he writes, "In the *maẕhab* of women there is no permission that she herself arise, or ask anyone to make preparations for the prayer, or even for her to move here and there herself. ..."[23] Such a juxtaposition—*maẕhab* and no prayer—makes its own point.

Custom Unveiled

How does Thānawī distinguish what is unacceptable practice? In the case of the first group of customs, those known to be sinful but considered minor, Thānawī's concern is to show how significant in fact the sin is. His method is to examine the actual custom and then to assess motivation and indirect consequences as well. The sins in this category are a diverse lot: watching dances and hearing music, playing with cards and kites, keeping dogs and pictures, and shaving part of the head. Dancing is treated most extensively and is shown to be the cause of a major sin, adultery. "All the men look at unrelated women: and that is adultery of the eyes. They hear their singing and talking: that is adultery of the ears. They talk with them: that is adultery of the tongue. If they incline their heart to them, that is adultery of the heart. Most offensive, they lay hands on them: that is adultery of the hands. They walk closer to them: that is adultery of the feet. Some even engage in fornication: that is real adultery."[24] The author goes on to show that the ills of such an act, and the resultant liability, also go far beyond the apparent misdeed. The person responsible for arranging the dancing is guilty of the sin of all the guests and should some guest choose to emulate the host on some future occasion, that sin, too, accrues to the original sinner. "Even after his or her death, as long as the chain keeps going, sin will accumulate in one's record of deeds."[25]

The sin is compounded here, as in so many other customary practices, by pride and by neglect of ritual obligations such as the canonical prayer. Here too there is "worldly harm," in this case that a husband or bridegroom may be distracted from loving his wife. Customs waste money. And some, like fireworks and kiteflying, even endanger lives. None of this category is singled out as regional or Hindu in origin. Although a Hindi word is used to describe the objectionable manner of keeping one's hair, it is simply condemned by referring to a *ḥadīth* forbidding partial shaving of the head.

The same kinds of arguments continue in the major section of the work, that which treats those customs considered wholly legitimate. Here the problem for the author is greater, for these are customs which "are performed from the time of coming into the world until one's dying breath. [People think] What sin is there in this? Men and women gather together; there is something to eat and drink; there is some exchange of gifts. There is no dancing; no throwing colors [as in the Hindu springtime festival of Holi]; no music. What goes against the Law and should be stopped?"[26]

Thus challenged, Thānawī, in the typical rationalizing style of the reformers, lists eleven principles against which to measure the seemingly endless and diverse customary practices associated with life-stage rituals:

1. Wasting of wealth
2. Motivation by desire for fame and glory
3. Requirement of gifts, feast, etc. which should be optional
4. Resemblance to practices of unbelievers
5. Necessitating of loans taken on interest or taken without need
6. Acceptance of gifts offered under compulsion
7. Violating seclusion
8. Polytheism and compromising belief
9. Missing prayer or performing it at a disapproved time
10. Aiding sin
11. Establishing a sinful custom and considering good what has been clearly denounced in Qurʾān and *ḥadīth.*[27]

The evil of each point is then confirmed by citations from the *ḥadīth.* Thānawī argues that the sinfulness of these customs is in fact neither subtle nor obscure although one must take into account attitudes and indirect consequences. There follows discussions of customary observances on the occasion of a child's birth; seven on shaving a child's head; five at the time of circumcision; nine upon the *biʾsmillāh* ceremony of beginning a child's education; eight to carry out an engagement; and no less than 103 for the marriage (*shādī*) itself. "*Shādī* [literally, joy] is,'' he writes, ''in reality, *barbādī* (ruin).''[28] To be saved from ruin, one must reflect on all customs and act accordingly.

Application of the Principles

As noted above, numerous principles are applied at great length to the exchanges of gifts and food that characterize life-cycle observances. Such exchanges include the gifts received from the invited guests, the gifts to daughters, and the rewards to menials, and are part of organizing structures of local society in north India as described by ethnographers throughout this past century. The practice of delayed reciprocity has been shown to be central in defining relationships beyond the immediate household and in providing resources for families in times of ritual or emergency need.[29] As described in the custom of *vartan bhānjī* for the Punjab, those invited to participate on some occasion are expected to bring a cash gift, slightly larger than that they last received, which then sets up an obligation on the part of the recipient to provide a gift to the giver on some future occasion. Information and control of these gifts appear to be largely in the hands of women and are a source of prestige and power for them within the family. Upon their appropriate discharge rests much of family status and resource in time of need. The term used for an invitation of this sort is *neʾotā* and it is regarded as a *ḥaqq*, an obligation upon the recipient.

Thānawī had no interest in the functional role of this practice in creating social bonds, let alone in cushioning the financial needs of those occasions of which he largely disapproved. He suggests that these customs had their origin as *inʿām* (spontaneous gifts given out of happiness) but that now their only purpose and intent (*nīyat* and *maqsūd*) is pride. The practice is objectionable on legal grounds of making something optional required. Moreover it violates the law of gifts by extracting gifts by force. Finally, it creates an illegitimate loan. This loan can only be repaid ceremonially instead of by the norms set for repayment, namely that one repay only if able and as soon as able. If a person tried to fulfill his *ḥaqq* on the next day, the payment would be refused.

> After the birth of the child, the women of the house gather along with other women of the family (*kuṅbā*) by invitation to offer something to the midwife. They do not give the money into her hand but throw it into a broken vessel. Now is this rational?... many of the women of the family may be impoverished or indigent. They, too, are implored to come. If they do not come, they are reproached their entire lives; and if they come and have not brought an eight-ānā or four-ānā bit, they are shamed and held in contempt.... What an outrage to invite a person and then loot her...! To come with an empty beak and just sit there! Why did she even bother to come?[30]

The giver, the recipient, and the people of the house are all equally implicated in sin.[31]

Customary gifts to daughters and sisters (*dhyānī*) are also condemned. On such occasions as a childbirth or circumcision, the maternal side of the family gives gifts, known as *bhāt*, which are incorporated into customary law (*ʿurf*) and considered the due (*ḥaqq*) of the daughters and sisters.[32] Here Thānawī recognizes the place of such gifts in the Hindu system and condemns them; both for their being Hindu and for their substituting for the legitimate system of inheritance in *sharīʿat* law. Thānawī comments:

> The real motive of *bhāt* is that the Hindus, upon the death of a father in Hindustan, give no share at all from his wealth to his daughters. Ignorant Muslims have adopted this line in emulation of them. And if they deny emulation and claim that they worked out this custom themselves, it is still wrong. How can it be right to deny, indeed to suppress, the inheritance right of a claimant established by God and his Messenger? When the girl was deprived of her inheritance, it was decided to satisfy her claims by gifts on different occasions and festivals.[33]

Recent ethnographic work on Hindus in the same area described by Maulānā Thānawī also elucidates concerns with auspiciousness attendant on the proper giving of gifts to those outside one's house [to *begānī*, stranger, as opposed to *apnī*, one's own son or daughter-in-law].[34] To give within the house would be inauspicious and would bring no benefit. Such concerns might be less salient to Muslims because concerns with auspiciousness presumably have less of a structuring role in their system of relationships and because marriage within families creates less of a clear demarcation between one's own and outsiders. The argument here mainly opposes these gifts as a substitute for adherence to the clear rules of *sharīʿat*-based inheritance.

In the same way gifts to menials in the course of ceremonies is identified as meaningful to Hindus but simply illegal for Muslims. These gifts were presumably part of patron-client reciprocity (*jajmānī*) in which services were rendered in return for periodic gifts from patrons.[35] In speaking of the primacy of gifts to the barber at weddings, Thānawī writes, "This is the custom of the Hindus. In their usage, the powers of the barber are very great and he therefore is highly valued. Ignorant Muslims have divested him of these powers but fix wages for him which are usually unjust...."[36] Elsewhere he mocks the custom by conflating it with *neʾotā*: "Why not give? The elders of this Sir Barber gave a loan to the ancestors of these poor people and now these unfortunate ones are repaying it lest their ancestors be obstructed from heaven! I take refuge in God...."[37] The gifts given to the menials are variously termed *chhatīs thāniyah*, *purōtā*, *neg*, *rīt*, and *bair ghaṛī*.[38] This last, given the bearer, Thānawī notes to be a Hindi word and learned from the infidels so that it is not only wrong in itself but is also a violation of order because of its origin.[39] Thānawī sums up these payments with the proverb, "In a marriage [nothing but] an account book of seed."[40]

These payments violate the legal requirements of both gifts and wages. A gift is an *iḥsān*, a kindness, to be given spontaneously and when one has the means.[41] Wages must be fixed in accordance with the specific job and set in advance to avoid their being *ijāra-yi fāsid*, a corrupt recompense.[42] A further objection is made to the bride's side and groom's side recompensing each other's servants. Innumerable distributions of food and sweets also take place, and these are considered illegitimate.

Other customs are denounced because they endanger health. Thānawī grows eloquent on the physical abuse of all-night weddings and feasting: "one person gets sick; another has indigestion; yet another, overcome by weariness, goes to sleep and misses his morning prayer."[43] *Sharbat* has to be drunk—a cooling substance in the indigenous system of food categories—even if the weather is cold or a guest is indisposed with a cold.

Other customs are omens or auspicious acts. Such customs are attempts to control God and to elicit knowledge of the unknown (*ᶜilmu 'l-ghaib*). A newborn child, for example, is swung in a winnowing basket, given certain plants, and protected by a sword and knife. Many customs are carried out by happily married wives (the *sāt suhāgan*) whose auspiciousness is of great power in Hindu thought. Also objectionable are non-Hindu customs like that of the groom's visit to a saintly shrine en route to collect the bride. The bride is sent home to her father's house on what are deemed to be inauspicious Muslim calendrical festivals such as the fasting month of Ramaẓān, the observance of *Shab-i Barāt* when one's prospects for the coming year are determined, and the mourning month of Muḥarram.

No worldly consideration is to stand in the way of ending all these practices. Thānawī suggests that the whole brotherhood might agree "that all this foolishness cease."[44] Otherwise one ought to begin alone. He is so confident that the benefits of this will be self-evident that he is sure even a single example will spread. He provides an example of a recent wedding based on the exemplary wedding of ᶜAlī and Fāṭima, a wedding of respectable people—not *maulawi* and *darwesh*, not poor, not lowly (*ćhotī qaum*).[45] He insists that the burden of proper action is greater on the rich since poor people in the brotherhood emulate them to protect their own honor. And he answers the objection that all this will put a cramp in conviviality. Conviviality after all cannot justify sin. Moreover, if visiting and giving gifts takes place without constraint, love and affection will flourish instead of the sorrow and wrangling that gatherings now encourage. But in fact, Thānawī considers these concerns irrelevant. He assumes that right doing will be irresistible to emulation; he knows that a good society will emerge if its component Muslims are good. Meanwhile even social disintegration could not intrude upon the unmistakably urgent task of fostering each Muslim's integrity before God.

The final section of the book outlines customs which are considered to be of positive religious merit but which in fact are illegitimate. They are in each case related to some ceremonial or religious observance such as *Fāṭiḥa* (the assignment of religious merit for some good work to the dead); calendrical observances like Ramaẓān, the two *ᶜĪd*s, and Muḥarram; and the veneration of relics. All have been overlaid with "foolishness added by the ignorant" and their practice, in echo of the "self-devised *sharīᶜat*" noted above, made into a *man gharat ṭarīqa* (a self-devised way of piety) here.[46]

For *Fāṭiḥa* one ought simply to assign the credit of a good deed like charity or Qurʾānic reading to the benefit of a dead person. Instead of this, however, ignorant people plaster the floor with mud, set out food including *pān* and water, and then have *sūras* of the Qur'ān read. In short, they create a *chauka*, the area spread with mud and cow dung where a Hindu cooks and eats his food, and then proceed to invite and feast the dead person. This is evident by the choice of the favorite foods of the deceased. At the least, this is an unnecesary elaboration and a distraction from normative observances. At worst, however, the ceremony is intended not only to transfer benefit to the dead but to invoke powerful figures of the past to come to one's aid. This then raises for the author the danger of *shirk*, of joining partners to God. Similar, he continues, is the practice of trying to remove illness by feeding meat to kites; by buying an animal and setting it free; and by placing food at the crossroads to placate a ghost. This he says, using the Hindu term, is worship (*pūjā*) of a created being and is the custom of the unbelievers. Having begun with what were deemed innocent peccadilloes, Thānawī has now reached what were considered a source of material and spiritual favor only to show that they are the most serious of sins that any Muslim, any human, can commit.

Control of Women and Self-Control

The elimination of customary practices meant a check on a major sphere of activity largely in the hands of women as well as restriction on the participation of women in gatherings and ceremonies that defined much of their social interaction and even identity. In the course of his second section, Thānawī interrupts his discussion of life-cycle rituals in order to digress at great length on the ills attending the participation of women in gatherings characteristic of virtually all the rituals.

His description, which extends to women going out in general, sketches a colorful vignette of women casting aside all restraint and gadding about day and night, by doli or even on foot. Off they go "to relatives or someone else, for weddings and condolence, for visiting the sick or joining a *barāt* [wedding procession]."[47] All is illegitimate, yet "nowhere in all Hindustan is the rule acted upon" that women ought go nowhere except on occasion to visit close relatives, and only then if no ceremony is planned.[48] He takes the reader through a chronology of an outing. First we see the news spreading that some ceremony is set in the *barādarī*, whereupon each woman sets out to devise some new and costly outfit. That sets in train the first chain of evils, for she starts dealing with strange men in the form of cloth merchants; she takes loans (with or without her husband's permission) and may even drive him to ill-gotten gains; she may buy gold or silver without knowing the complexities of such transactions. Through all her only motive is pride and display, condemned in Qur'ān and *ḥadīth.* She may even borrow jewelry and try to pass it off as her own.

Finally ready, she summons a doli. At that point milady thinks to take a bath. Off she goes, the doli kept waiting, the canonical prayer missed, the lady made late, whereupon she starts cursing the hapless *kahār*. Out she rushes, muttering, "God, God" (*khudā khudā kar kē*), pushes aside the *kahār* and gets herself in. Parts of her dress are on display; the curtain may even be open; maybe her perfume excites interest along the way.

At last she arrives and runs in, taking no thought that she might inquire ahead to avoid colliding with strange men. She greets the other women but there is no exchange of the requisite *as-salāmu ʿalaikum*. She simply touches her hand to her forehead or says a quick *salām*. The answers given back in turn are all derived from local custom: "Keep cool" (a reference to the hot and cold continuum in which one hopes to be restrained and peaceful); "Live on!"; "May you remain a beloved wife" (the auspicious *suhāgan* of Hinduism); "May you bathe in milk and bear many children" (the first a wish for the many cattle which are a source to Indians of both wealth and auspiciousness); "May your brother/husband/children live."[49] The greeting is only the beginning. Then begins what the author believes to be the substance of feminine conversation: gossip, complaint, backbiting, slander and reproach, all set to a choreography of display of one's own dress on the one hand and judgment of the dress of others on the other. This sets in train a list of classical sins: envy, ingratitude, desire, and pride. Meanwhile the male *sāqī* and older sons of the household wander about. The meal is served and a tempest begins as each woman attacks the food in the company of the parasites she has brought along with no concern for the people of the house.

This over, the exit begins. The women hear the sound of the dolis and "like Gog and Magog, one on top of the other, all are crushed at the door trying to be the first to get a ride." They pile in, sometimes sneaking two into the doli to cheat the *kahār*. Someone loses something and a good row is started as unjust blame is laid. Meanwhile the men are standing around watching the show. For days afterward "the worms" continue to wiggle as days are spent in assessing who came and how, and what arrangments were made by the hostess. Thus the author has listed thirty-two separate sins in all this and warns that these are only a few of those that actually happen! The puritan standards of outward observance of the Law and inward moral purification and control could not be more challenged.

At the center of the reformist vision of the proper Muslim life are implicit theories of self-control and of discipline by reason (*ʿaql*), in the sense of rational discrimination of divine law, and subsequent control of the lower and wilful self (*nafs*).[50] Women, in general, are thought capable of the same discipline and transformation as men. The positive view of women is reflected in the biographies of good women in the *Bihishtī Zewar* and in the section on personal development. At this level, men's attempts to influence or control women can be seen not as oppression but simply as extending to women, too, the opportunity to exercise the kind of control over themselves that is at the base of their too becoming fully human.

Yet the anxiety over women's behavior, as reflected in the description above, suggests an element of psychodrama in which women are seen as an extension of men. In the culture generally women are associated with *nafs*, both as a stimulus to male lack of control and as metaphor.[51] Thānawī himself is ambivalent about women, for while the major thrust of the book is to insist upon women's potential for control, in sections like those on outings he thinks of women as lacking in control, as not *maᶜqūl* (rational). Since the regional culture, moreover, when called into question as it is here, can also be equated with *nafs* as less disciplined and less ordered,[52] the high seriousness given to the end of custom can be understood. In custom the reformers' conceptions of women and the region come together. To control women (who are preeminently responsible for carrying out local customary practices) is to control oneself.

It is in the context of their individual personal ideals that the reformers' lively concern with a correct interpretation of Islam must be seen. In the demographic and political situation of British India, Muslims were stimulated to a concern with creating religiously informed, highly self-controlled, and responsible individuals. To this end, they felt constrained to inveigh against all family- and locally oriented, customarily sanctioned, ceremonies and observances as violations of injunctions of scripture; occasions for frivolity, if not licentiousness; and as distractions toward family involvements that interfered with relations to teachers who pointed one to the correct, all-important relationships to the Prophet and to God. The debate took place in a local context. But the kinds of tensions, the forms of argument, the attention to central symbols, and the process of change are ones that have periodically linked Muslims to each other across space and throughout history.

NOTES

1 I am very grateful to Sandria Freitag, David Gilmartin, Thomas Metcalf, and Laurel Steele who read a first draft of this paper with their customary good humor and insight; to Ira Lapidus, for on-going discussions on these issues over many months; and to Peter Brown, in absentia, for the inspiration provided by *The Cult of the Saints: Its Rise and Function in Latin Christianity* (Chicago: University of Chicago Press, 1981) as I was finishing this paper. I am also endebted to the Translation Grants Program of the National Endowment for the Humanities for their generous support to prepare a translation of the *Bihishtī Zewar* on which much of this paper is based. References to the *Bihishtī Zewar* below (after first citation simply "Book" and page) are to the edition of the British Library catalogued under Thānawī and dated 1906 (although in fact it contains the earliest editions of the sections published in various years about that time. Later editions are available in PL 480 collections in this country not only in Urdu but in translations to Pushtu, Bengali, and even (albeit partial and unclear) English.

2 *Bihishtī Zewar*, Book VIII, p. 51.

3 See Peter Brown, *The Cult of the Saints*, pp. 12-20.

4 For a stimulating discussion of what is normative in Islam see Jacques Waardenburg, "Islamic Studies, and the History of Religions: An Evaluation," in Richard C. Martin, ed., *Islam and the History of Religions: Perspectives on the Study of a Religious Tradition* (Berkeley, Calif.: Berkeley Religious Studies Series [forthcoming]).

5 See my *Islamic Revival in British India: the Deobandi ᶜUlama, 1860-1900* (Princeton: Princeton University Press, [1982]).

6 For this larger understanding of reason in Western culture, see C. S. Lewis, *The Discarded Image: An Introduction to Medieval and Renaissance Literature* (Cambridge: Cambridge University Press, 1964).

7 *Bihishtī Zewar*, Book VI, p. 3.

8 Book VI, p. 26.
9 Book VI, p. 10.
10 Book VI, p. 6.
11 Book VI, p. 13.
12 Book VI, p. 4.
13 Book VI, p. 40.
14 Book VI, p. 43.
15 Book VI, p. 27.
16 Book VI, p. 30.
17 Book VI, p. 16.
18 Book VI, p. 40.
19 Book VI, p. 46.
20 Book VI, p. 45.
21 Book VI, p. 28.
22 Book VI, p. 36.
23 Book VI, p. 46.
24 Book VI, p. 2.
25 Book VI, p. 3.
26 Book VI, p. 6.
27 Book VI, p. 52.
28 Book VI, p. 28.
29 See Zekiye S. Eglar, *A Punjabi Village in Pakistan* (New York: Columbia University Press, 1960) and H. A. Alavi, "Kinship in West Pakistan Villages," in T. N. Madan, ed., *Muslim Communities of South Asia* (New Delhi: Vicas Publishing House, ca. 1976), pp. 1-27.
30 Book VI, p. 8.
31 This discussion of *neʾotā* is notable for defining the circle included as *kunba* whereas other discussions of rural reciprocity describe larger circles of association; and also for suggesting that the amount may be variable (in this passage, "an eight-anna or four-anna bit").
32 Book VI, pp. 17, 15.
33 Book VI, p. 17.
34 This is discussed in the forthcoming dissertation by Gloria Raheja for the Department of Anthropology, University of Chicago.
35 See William H. Wiser and Charlotte V. Wiser, *Behind Mud Walls, 1930-1960* (Berkeley: University of California Press, 1971 [1951]) and William H. Wiser, *The Hindu Jajmani System* (Lucknow: Lucknow Publishing House, 1958 [1936]). The same village studied by the pioneer Wisers has recently been revisited and analyzed by anthropologists Susan Wadley and Bruce Derr.
36 Book VI, p. 49.
37 Book VI, p. 38.
38 The following definitions are provided by the contemporaneous John T. Platts, *A Dictionary of Urdu, Classical Hindi and English* (Delhi, 1884; reprint 1977). *Purōtā*: presents (of flour, sugar, turmeric, etc.) given at marriages to the barber, laundress, etc.; *rīt*: general course or way, method, mode, manner, observance custom; *neg*: established custom, usage rule; privilege, the customary presents at marriage and on other festive occasions made to relatives and dependents (and considered by them as perquisites to which they are entitled).
39 Book VI, p. 37.
40 Book VI, p. 40.
41 Book VI, p. 11.
42 Book VI, p. 35.
43 Book VI, p. 37.
44 Book VI, p. 54.
45 Book VI, p. 60.
46 Book VI, p. 64.
47 Book VI, p. 20.
48 Book VI, p. 20.

49 Book VI, p. 23.

50 These theories are explored in my edited volume *Moral Conduct and Authority: The Place of Adab in South Asian Islam* (Berkeley and Los Angeles: University of California Press, forthcoming), especially in articles by Ira M. Lapidus, Richard Kurin, Dr. Muhammad Ajmal, and myself.

51 For this perspective in another Muslim culture see James T. Siegel, *The Rope of God* (Berkeley and Los Angeles: University of California Press, 1969).

52 For this concept in the Punjab see Richard Kurin, ''Conflicting Valuations of Personhood in Two Pakistani Communities'' (a paper presented at the conference South Asian Islam, Moral Principles in Tension, Pendle Hill, May 22-25, 1981) where Punjabi culture is seen as more impulsive, more childlike; and for thirteenth-century Punjabi poetry where one symbol of the *nafs* is the Hindu, and the world of clay and darkness (in contrast to Turkestan) is Hindustan, see Annemarie Schimmel, *The Triumphal Sun: A Study in the Works of Jalaloddin Rumi* (Boulder, Colo.: Great Eastern, 1978).

Contributions to Asian Studies, Vol. XVII

Islam in the Chinese Environment

RAPHAEL ISRAELI
The Hebrew University of Jerusalem, Israel

Historical Background

ISLAM CAME TO CHINA as early as the Tang period (seventh-ninth centuries), probably during the eighth century. The first Muslim settlers in China were Arab and Persian merchants who traveled via the sea routes around India and soon found the Chinese trade remunerative enough to justify their permanent presence in Chinese coastal cities. In those days, the Muslims dwelled apart in separate quarters and actually maintained the Muslim mode of life which they had imported with them, and this seclusion was facilitated by the almost extra-territorial rights they enjoyed. They preserved their Arabic names, their original dress, their Persian and Arabic tongues, and conducted their religious and social life independently of the Chinese. Moreover, many of them married Chinese women or bought Chinese children in times of famine, thus not only consciously contributing to the numerical growth of the Muslim community, but also unwittingly injecting into their midst the first germ of their ultimate ethnic assimilation.

The Yuan rule in China (1279-1368) considerably boosted Muslim existence in the Middle Kingdom inasmuch as the Muslims, together with other non-Chinese groups (*simu*) were superimposed by the Mongol conqueror upon the Chinese. The Muslims, both those who had settled in China in previous centuries and the newly-arrived allies of the Mongols from the Muslim sultanates of Central Asia, indeed wielded a great deal of power, the most prominent example being Sayyid Edjell who conquered Yunnan for the Yuan and was nominated by the Khan as the first governor of that province. The borders of Central Asia being wide-open for trade and ideas during the Mongol rule, considerable numbers of Muslims moved to settle in the northwestern and southwestern provinces of China, and strong ties were established and cultivated between the Muslims of China and the lands of Islam.

The retrenchment of the Ming (1368-1644) and the self-isolation that came as a reaction to the rule of the Mongol barbarians over China constituted a major watershed in the fortunes of Chinese Muslims. From then on, one could indeed speak of "Chinese Muslims" and no longer about "Muslims in China." The Muslims adopted Chinese names, became fluent in Chinese, and in most cases, at least as far as China proper was concerned, they became outwardly undistinguishable from the Chinese. This same trend continued throughout the "High Qing," that is until the end of the Qianlong reign (A.D. 1796).

The decline of the Manchu Dynasty which was accompanied by the symptomatic plights of demographic explosion, scarcity of resources, devolution of power, and the rise of anti-establishment groups such as secret societies, was, in this instance, also coupled with a startling Muslim revivalist movement in China. This movement, which gathered momentum during the 19th Century, was contemporaneous with a similar outburst of Muslim fundamentalism in India, known as the *wahhābiyya*, and was generated by the spread of the Naqshbandi Sufi Order from Central Asia into China. The most dramatic development resulting from this movement was the *avant-garde* role that the "New Sect" of Chinese Islam played in Muslim rebellions during the final years of the Qing. Indeed, the Muslim revolts of the mid-nineteenth century which threw most of China's northwest and southwest into chaos, were apparently connected with the "New Sectarians."

The Muslim revolts were in the main initiated in provinces where the Muslims constituted a large portion of the population. In Gansu, the rebellion was led by the messianic figure of Ma Hualong, who attempted to establish a Muslin state, during the 1850s and 1860s but it ended in failure. In Yunnan, Du Wenxiu proclaimed himself "Sultan Suleiman" and governed a secessionist Muslim state for about sixteen years (1856-1872) before he succombed to the Imperial forces. The same fate awaited the Sinkiang revolt of the Uighur Muslims (in the 1870s). But although these rebellions were quelled, amidst a terrifying bloodshed, the Muslims never gave up either their separate identity as Muslims or their messianic craving for a schism from the Chinese polity if and when the opportunity should arise. Indeed, some outbursts of Muslim secessionism were recorded at the turn of the century, and again during the communist rule when the Hundred Flowers campaign of the mid-1950s was proclaimed.

The Anthropological Setting

The relationship between the Chinese majority and the Muslim (Hui) minority in China must be conceived in terms of interaction between two different groups, each with its own fears, suspicions, stereotypes (real or imaginary), and way of life. The Chinese Muslims, by following their dietary laws, praying in their separate mosques, holding on to their own calendar, and living in their closely knit communities, *eo ipso* set themselves apart from the Chinese, confident of their superiority and proud of their distinctiveness. The Chinese, ignorant of the underlying religious and cultural necessity for this self-imposed isolation, could not help but despise and ridicule those who lived in the heart of civilization but were unwilling to partake of its benefits. Ancestor worship, for example, the very pivot of Chinese culture and tradition, was not practised by the Muslims. On what common ground, then, could Muslims and Chinese meet?

The encounter in China of the enormously self-confident Chinese and Islamic cultures on a majority-minority basis and the resulting problems, ranging from acculturation to confrontation, can be analyzed as a three-phased process of cultural change.

The first phase is that in which "normal" conditions prevail, namely an ostensibly peaceful coexistence between the two cultures, with each side confident of its superiority, to be sure, but avoiding a head-on collision. Due to the constant diffusion of Chinese cultural elements into the Islamic community on the one hand, and the exclusive nature of Islam on the other, Chinese Muslims were subjected to two contradictory pressures: the pressure of the assimilatory factor pushing them to acculturate to the Chinese majority culture, and the pressure of the cultural specific pulling them to preserve the core of their culture and identity as Muslims. As long as the balance between the two could be maintained, Chinese Muslim society had adequate mechanisms for keeping chronic stress at a tolerable level.

As a general rule, in contact between cultures, material objects are taken over by the guest culture earlier than non-material characteristics. Tools and clothing, for example, are adopted by the recipient culture before religious ideas and social organizations. Chinese Muslims, under the stress of the assimilatory factor, were responsive mainly to the Chinese material culture but stopped short of spiritual or ideological acculturation. Their mosques borrowed the outside appearance of Chinese temples; their clothing, speech and manners became Chinese. But the core of Muslim doctrine and practice seems to have remained intact as far as the mainstream of Islam was concerned. To the extent that Muslim scholars attempted to present Islam to the Chinese as a close relative of Confucianism, they did so apologetically, not as a genuine expression of their own ideas and beliefs, but rather to ease the outside pressure by bridging the gap between themselves and the Chinese on the intellectual level.

In this setting, where cultural contact results in an almost unidirectional diffusion from the dominant to the recipient culture, and social interaction generates strong internal pressures for self-identity, a peculiar pattern of behaviour was adopted by the guest culture. Outwardly, they behaved like Chinese, spoke Chinese, called each other by their Chinese names and wore Chinese clothing. But inwardly they behaved like Muslims, put on special items of clothing for prayer, greeted each other in Arabic, called each other by their Arabic names, turned to Mecca for prayer and maintained a high degree of social cohesion. In short, their behaviour had an adaptive significance insofar as they attempted to be Chinese outdoors and Muslim indoors.

The second phase set in when the intensification of outside pressure on the part of the host culture was counteracted by a parallel intensification of internal pressure within the guest culture. This process was more likely to take place in areas containing the largest proportions of minority groups. In these regions discrimination and persecution against the minority were more acute, for this group constituted a major threat to the political, economic and social position of the majority. As a result of mutual prejudice and discrimination, both the majority and the minority developed a heightened awareness of the minority's distinguishing characteristics, which led to stereotyping and its corollaries—suspicion and hostility on both sides.

The responses typically open to a minority group in this situation are avoidance of contact, acceptance of the situation, or aggression against it. In the case of the Chinese Muslims, the first possibility was not always feasible, due to the social interdependence and the unavoidable Muslim dependence on the Chinese political order and bureaucratic system. The second type of response, acceptance of the situation, is prevalent in the first phase and is exemplified in the Muslim attempts to acculturate materially and accommodate outwardly with the host culture. But when the stress of discrimination became intolerable, the balance between inner and outer pressures was upset and the minority resorted to the third type of response: aggression or rebellion.

In this phase, which was characterized by violent antagonism between the host and guest cultures, there developed an extreme ideological polarization. In China, very significantly, the Muslims turned to mystical and messianic Islamic doctrines. The rebellion was not solely an outburst of rage or a mere necessity of physical survival, but was the only way open to the Muslim minority to reassert its cultural identity, free from the pressures of the dominant culture.

As in the case of Yunnan, the third phase was contingent upon the at least temporary success of the rebellion. With Muslim autonomy won and a Muslim independent political entity established, the Muslim minority became dominant over the Chinese majority. Islam, though still the minority culture, became the state religion and the culture of the ruling elite. In their attempt to reassert their identity, the Muslims, now masters of their own fate, tended overtly to return to their cultural roots and revive Muslim traditions relating to statehood that had survived in their historical memory but could never be articulated in the midst of a hostile cultural majority.

With the establishment of an Islamic state, the Muslims were confronted with dilemmas such as whether they should impose their culture on the Chinese majority or, because of practical considerations of government, they should seek to accommodate the Chinese population in order to mitigate the antagonism of the past and gain popular support. The solutions of Pingnan Quo, Du Wenxiu's state in Yunnan, were reflected in the state's religious symbols, the state administration, a new stratification of society, taxation, and the like. If the state were to be Islamic, what role should the non-Muslims play in it? What might be their status vis-à-vis their Muslim masters? What law applied to them, the Chinese or the Islamic? Are they a tolerated cultural group or should they be induced, if not compelled, to embrace Islam? What part of the Chinese system of law and administration, if any at all, should be preserved? Should the traditional scholar bureaucracy be incorporated into the new regime or should a novel elite be substituted for it? The inadequate solutions to these dilemmas contributed, in part, to the collapse of the Muslim independent state in Yunnan in the face of the counterattacks launched by the Qing Dynasty at the height of the Tongzhi Restoration.

After the failure of the secessionist alternative, the Muslims reverted to a constant swing between the first and second phases, namely, from "normal" uneasy coexistence in times of relative peace, to antagonism and open rebellion when Chinese pressures made life impossible for Muslims. The third phase of seclusion and political autonomy is yet to reproduce itself.

Chinese Versus Muslims

Intellectually as well as practically, the Chinese of the Confucian tradition could hardly tolerate a guest culture such as that of the Muslims in their midst. This is all the more so under the communist regime of contemporary China, the best evidence for that being the generally harsh policy of the Peking regime towards the minorities in general and the Muslims in particular.

In traditional China the reasons for this uneasy coexistence could be identified mainly in the wide intellectual hiatus that separated the two communities. In fact, the Muslims differed from all other minority groups in that, although they were concentrated mainly in marginal areas of the Empire, they were present in virtually every province and every sizable urban agglomeration throughout the country, and their presence was not merely statistical. They had large communities in the capitals (Nanjing and Beijing), they handled some trade in many places, and left their impact (though more as individuals than as a collective) all over the place. This may explain the ubiquitous nature of the hatred, jealousy and contempt in which they were held by the Chinese at large. Conversely, from the authorities' point of view, no crash program in a certain territory could force all the Hui to acculturate, since there was no such single territory. For this reason, while the other major minorities were handled under the Qing by the Li Fanyuan, which controlled them by controlling their territory, the Hui were free from such control.

Secondly, since the Muslims could not accept the principle of filial piety and participate in the ceremonies of the Ancestral Shrines in the Court, through which the Chinese attempted to "civilize" non-Chinese barbarians, they chose to remain outside the pale of the sought-for "refinement and virtue." Neither was the stratagem that the Qing used with non-Chinese aborigines workable with the Muslims. The Hui had their own sense of superiority, their own festivals and religious symbolism, their own learning and culture, and needed no "uplifting" to the heights of Chinese civilization. In short, they did not yield to the *mission civilisatrice* of their Chinese hosts. The result was, as an eyewitness missionary remarked, that "close contact with this people has given convincing proof that the line of demarcation between Muslim and non-Muslim Chinese is as great as, if not greater than, that between Chinese and foreigners.... Although the Muslims have had, in one sense, to conform to Chinese law, there is another sense in which they are always a law unto themselves. The profound teachings of Buddha and Confucius are nothing to them."[1]

From a Chinese intellectual's point of view, then, if Confucius means nothing to the Muslims, this signifies that they are outside the pale of civilization. More specifically, if they lack adherence to the Confucian principle of filial piety, as exemplified in their ignorance of ancestor worship, then all the socio-political and religio-ethical tenets that bind the Chinese together do not obtain for Muslims. That is to say, **a)** If Muslims are outside the framework of the father-son relationship, then they are bound to be unruly vis-à-vis their family hierarchy, the local authority and even the emperor. As such, they are detrimental, at least potentially, to the social order in particular and to the Chinese polity in general. **b)** If Muslims do not respect the rituals due to ancestors and other spirits, they are exposed to the malicious deeds of those spirits, and thus one had better keep away from them. **c)** If the blessings of heaven are transmitted to earth through the Son of Heaven, the Muslims, by being unfilial to the emperor, cannot rejoice in those blessings and thus cannot partake of Chinese civilization. **d)** Since the emperor, though claiming no superiority over heaven, is the ruler of both temporal and celestial orders, the Muslims, claiming that celestial powers are beyond the emperor's authority, are likely to fall short of respecting the Chinese monarch and what he represents. How, then, can they be expected to be his loyal subjects? **e)** In general, ancestor worship and filial piety imply the acceptance of the Ways of the Ancients. If the Muslims have their own calendar, celebrate their own festivals, have no attachment to their locale of domicile, and pay no attention to the Chinese Way, how can they be considered Chinese?

Indeed, in the eyes of the thinking Chinese literati, who would formulate their objections to Muslims in intellectual and rational terms, the gap between the two communities might have looked so hopelessly unbridgeable that they could easily come under the sway of popular stereotypes, which tended to make the gap look even wider.

These stereotypes, which grew to be grossly exaggerated misjudgments of the Muslims by the Chinese, were constantly fed by the alienation between the two communities, as reflected in contemptuous name-calling, vicious storytelling and eventually in pogrom-style onslaughts when the opportunity presented itself.

One may try to trace the origins of the anti-Muslim sentiment in China to the times of the Yuan Dynasty (1279-1368), when Muslims from central and western Asia were brought *en masse* by the Mongols to China as a sort of civil service that was imposed at the top of Chinese society. Understandably, the Chinese must have identified Muslims (Saracens, in Medieval European parlance) with their conquerors and oppressors. Marco Polo recorded:

> All the Cathaians detested the great Khan's rule because he set over them governors who were Tartars, and still more frequently Saracens, and these they could not endure, for they were treated by them like slaves. You see, the Great Khan had not succeeded to the dominion of Cathay by hereditary right but held it by conquest; and thus, having no confidence in the natives, he put all authority in the hands of Tartars, Saracens, and Christians, who were attached to his household and devoted to his service, and were themselves foreigners in Cathay.[2]

Such Chinese sentiments must have been reinforced by the fact that Muslims were assigned special sections in the cities where they settled, where they enjoyed virtual extraterritorial privileges. Ibn Baṭṭūṭa, who visited China in 1342, recorded that the dissonance between the Muslim sections in the cities and the Chinese sections was so great that "the markets in the Muslim sections are similar to those in Muslim lands. In the cities there are mosques and *muazzins*, we heard them calling for prayer."[3]

Deep-seated mistrust, once thoroughly established, tended to become self-perpetuating and to generate, for one, a gross misjudgment of the Muslim community by way of stereotype and rationalization. This situation is not unlike the fantastic stories circulated among the Chinese about the Westerners during and subsequent to the Opium War. In the latter case, hostility towards Christianity and missionary work in China was, to a large extent, a result of popular resentment of the West of the different type of life that the Europeans developed in the Treaty Ports.

Whatever the origins of prejudice, it is evident that with the spread of Islam in China, more and more Chinese in the hinterland came into contact with Muslim communities so that the stereotypes regarding Muslims becamе almost universal. In popular conception the Muslim was portrayed as savage, heartless, aggressive and a greedy creature, capable of the most horrible crimes to achieve his goals. A story that became a legend in Northern China relates that "during the season of the Chinese New Year, Muslims, who do not observe the same festival, invited the Chinese in their caravan to make merry, while they would stand the night watch. After the Chinese were drunk, the Muslims rose up, pulled their tent down on them and beat them to death under it. Then they threw the bodies into a dry well and made off with the silver. The murder was not discovered until next spring. It made a great stir, being one of the most savage crimes ever committed in the region."[4]
There is no way to ascertain whether this story is authentic or not. But its stereotypical nature is obvious, and where stereotypes are concerned, it is popular belief, not genuine fact, that matters. Another popular stereotype is that Muslims do not take their religion in earnest, implying that this whole affair of *Qingzhen jiao* (Pure and True Religion), as the Muslims term their faith, is pure hypocrisy. They also believe that a Muslim would take care to respect his religion only in the presence of other Muslims. The Chinese proverb says: "Three Muslims are one Muslim; two Muslims are half a Muslim; one Muslim is no Muslim."[5] Consider another example.

> A Muslim traveler reached a town at night.
> "What meat do you have there?" he asked the inn-keeper, pointing to a tray of hot meat patties.
> "Pork" said the Chinese.
> "Ah", he said, "and what is that?", pointing to another row of the same patties.
> "Pork, of course," said the Chinese.
> "And these", persisted the Muslim, pointing to a third row.
> The food-seller, exasperated, muttered: "These are mutton."
> "Well, why did you not say that before?" and he began to eat heartily.[6]

Another gibe went as follows: one Muslim traveling will grow fat, two on a journey will become thin,[7] the inference being that one will eat pork while two dare not.

Muslims are taken to be selfish and greedy, which of course reinforces Chinese dislike and contempt for them. The following incident was viewed by Owen Lattimore while he was traveling with a mixed Chinese-Muslim caravan in North China: "Mohammedans broke off from the caravan to get first to the water well at the edge of the desert. The Chinese cursed them heartily, there being little affection between the Great and Little Faiths, saying that they had gone ahead when it was to their advantage, but would cling to us from now on, for the sake of company through the country where there is danger or raiders."[8]

The Muslims were credited by the Chinese with courage, energy and enterprise, and were said to be persuasive in talk and in blarney, but they were maligned for being too shrewd and sly to be dependable in business. The proverb goes: "eat the food of a Muslim but do not listen to his talk,"[9] meaning take what he offers but do not believe what he promises. Another popular saying: "Ten Peking [Beijing] slippery ones cannot talk down one Tientsin [Tianjin] brawler, ten Tientsin brawlers cannot talk down one Muslim."[10]

The Chinese talked about Muslims the way the English talk about the Irish and anti-Semites talk about Jews, so even admirable qualities inherent in them or in their culture are deprecated. Courage and energy are said to be channeled to evil ends; shrewdness is interpreted as slyness; and persuasive talking is seen as flattery. Even the proverbial cleanliness of the Muslims, attested to by all foreign observers, to the extent that a missionary called them "the Clean Sect in China," was brushed aside and interpreted as "another way of life" rather than a characteristic with its intrinsic value. "Of course," the Chinese would say, "his house is cleaner than mine, he is a Muslim."

The fashion in which the Chinese addressed Muslims or referred to them is another interesting facet of the relationship between these two groups. There were both "neutral" (as opposed to polite) and overtly contemptuous references, the one being used generally in the presence of Muslims, the other in their absence. Honorable addresses were hardly ever used. The common term by which Muslims have traditionally been known in China, from the Yuan on, is *Hui*, or *Huihui*, and the religion was referred to as the *Huijiao* (The Hui Sect). There are various theories regarding the origin of these terms, some more fantastic than others. Suffice it to say that this term did not refer exclusively to Muslims but to Jews and some Christians too. Deviations from these standard terms by Chinese ranged all the way from demeaning diminutives to contemptuous nicknames, even to slanderous insults. *Huizi* is not exactly a respectful reference, unlike *Laohui* which one could use if one wished to show respect. The Chinese also termed Islam *Xiaojiao* (Little Doctrine), as opposed to the Chinese who had the *Dajiao* (Great Doctrine). Incidentally, the Chinese are said to have assigned to themselves the *Dajiao* only to indicate their non-belonging to any particular sect. Another way of setting

Islam apart was to refer to it as *jiejiao*, literally, in this context, "the Doctrine apart" or the "different Doctrine."

It is evident that Chinese Muslims were prone to be insulted by all of these references to them, and that they therefore adopted the formal title of Qingzhen jiao" (Pure and True Religion), which is inscribed over the gates of the mosques and used in communications between Muslims. This term, like much of the Muslim liturgical terminology, was apparently borrowed from Chinese Jews.

All this hostility was, of course, constantly fed by the ever present gap between the two groups. Religion in China was closely intertwined with intellectual life and with the political and social institutions of the nation. Confucianism was identified with scholarship and was deeply entrenched in the habits of thought, affections, and loyalties of the educated people. The state was committed to the existing faiths, especially Confucianism. Confucian classics were the basis for education and the examination system. Ceremonies were associated with Confucianism and maintained at public expense. Officials, including the emperor, performed many of the duties usually assigned to a priesthood in other cultures. The very political theory on which the state rested derived its authority from Confucian teachings.

Religion also formed part of the village life. Temples were maintained by villages, and festivals and ceremonies took place through general contribution. Guilds had patron Gods and other religious features. Above all, the family, the strongest social unit, had as an integral part of its structure the honoring of ancestors by rites that were religious in origin and retained a religious significance. Muslims were out of place in this setting, since their social and religious norms were so different and could not displace the already well-entrenched Chinese philosophies and traditions. They went their own ways, in prayers and ceremonies, in their calendar and festivals, in their weddings and burial of the dead, in their socializing and eating habits, in their traveling and dwelling. So, no matter how much the Muslims wished to put on an appearance of being Chinese they were and remained Hui people, that is non-Chinese, in the eyes of the Chinese.

Chinese Muslims, for their part, felt they were alien people, more akin to other members of the world Muslim community—the *umma*—than to their Chinese neighbors. Their main concern being their religion, and their identity being focused on the universal *umma*, the deeply ingrained Chinese tradition of identification with the locus of domicile did not obtain with them. The specific congregation to which a Muslim belonged had for him a functional and temporary quality, not the intrinsic and immutable value that the Chinese felt for his village, country and province. For the Chinese, attachment to the locale was part of the way of his ancestors. His life and death in the locale were irrevocably tied up with the local spirits whose protection he sought, and the geomancy that he could not disturb. This deep identification with the locale was instrumental in the development not only of local patriotism, but also of the spirit of association (*hui*) among the Chinese. Ask any Chinese about his homeland, and he will most probably give you the name of his county and province. Chinese originating from the same province or county will find each other when they live or travel outside their provinces, within or outside China, and form associations on that basis (*tongxiang hui*).

The link between the local and the universal was provided by the literati, who had provincial ties and local commitments, but were at the same time the owners of the high culture that transcended the locale and encompassed *tianxia*, the whole civilized world. Levenson has aptly remarked that "such ties were part of, not rival to, ecumenical Confucianism, transprovincial, or worldly and cosmopolitan. These ties formed part of the personal-relationship ambiance of Confucianism."[11] Chinese gentry played the double role of local social leaders and also of a trained, skilled, educated and indoctrinated pool of potential officials of the empire. In both roles, the literati were acknowledged as superior men who knew how to manage society, knew the proper rules of conduct, and could apply the ethical tenets of Confucianism to both the operation of the state and the affairs of the people. In this capacity, they provided the link between state and society. Thus, the gentry officials, while serving the emperor, were at the same time in opposition to him as champions of local interests. Local interests were not only economic (as landlords) but also social (as members of clans and lineages).

Because of the prestige that their Confucian training gave them, sanctioned by the state examination system, they filled various social functions that reflected both their ethical commitment to the system, as *junzi*, and their social commitment as members of their clans and leaders of their communities. They acted as arbitrators in local conflicts, took care of the poor and the weak, organized charity and relief in times of calamity, and supervised education. In other words, their state-sponsored Confucian training gave them the knowledge of the moral code that was essential for the operation of society, while their function in society provided the state with the stability and continuity in local government. It was the balanced tension between these two poles which enabled the hierarchical system to function effectively.

It is precisely this balance that breaks down in the relationship between the Confucian state and Muslim communities in China. The Muslim elite, i.e. the Imams, who managed the affairs of the Muslim community in the fields of social welfare, arbitration of disputes and education, were religious figures whose ideology, far from thriving on symbiotic coexistence with the state, was in many ways antithetical to it. Their commitment to the community was not ordained by a social status sanctioned by the state, but by an elective office they gained through their knowledge. Their knowledge of Islam, though universal in import, was acknowledge only by their local community.

For the Chinese Muslim, the local congregation provided the framework of his life and the focus of his identity. But at the same time he realized that this was only part of the universal *umma*. Since the *umma* had, from its very inception, the dual character of a political as well as a religious organization, the Chinese Muslim could sublimate through it his political frustration in China and his political aspirations outside of it. Similarly, since the Muslim had no mystical attachment to his locus of domicile, he substituted for it Arabia, the holy place of inception of the *umma*, or other loci of significance to Muslims.

Mr. Morrison, a traveler in China at the beginning of the nineteenth century, related the following: "On the evening of Sept. 10, whilst walking on shore at a village called T'u-liao [Tuliao], about fifty miles from Tientsin [Tianjin], I observed written on the lantern of a poor huckster's shop, 'A Mohammedan shop.' On stopping to ask the owner, who was an old man, whence he came, he replied: 'From Hsi yang' [Xiyang] (The Western Ocean). When urged to say what country of the West, he said he did not know. He understood his family had been in the place for five generations."[12] The old man's family had been there for five generations, but *he* had come from the Western Ocean. Owen Lattimore, a century later, encountered the same phenomenon during his travel to Inner Mongolia. "The talk turned on to the Muhammedans. Some said that *their* holy city is west of Turkestan. One of them said that he had heard the "Turbaned-Heads" (Muslims) speak of it, they called it Rum."[13]

In Chinese Muslim literature since 1642 (none is known to have been written prior to that date), the centrality of Arabia was a current theme. *Tianfang* (The Celestial Area) was the Chinese word for the land of the Prophet. One Muslim author of the seventeenth century boasted about his ancestors being from *Tjanfang*. Another author entitled his treatise about Islam *Tianfang dianli* (Rituals of Arabia). Still another wrote: "Arabia, not China, is the center of the world. Fu-hsi [Fuxi], the first legendary monarch of China, was a descendant of Adam who came from the West.[14]

The Arabic alphabet, the sacred script of the Holy Qurʾān, was by derivation referred to as *Tianfang zimu* (Arabia's Characters). Since the Muslims in China were under the rule of the heathen, and thus unable to put into practice the political aspects of the ideal of the *umma*, they were in a dilemma as to how they should conduct themselves. Were they to rebel or to accept the yoke of their rulers? What was the limit of infringements on the borders of the *umma* that they could tolerate? In case the situation became intolerable, to whom should they turn? Should they dissipate their frustration and wait for the *Dushi* (The Great Enterprise) that sectarian groups in China had always been waiting for? The solutions to these problems were sought in the framework of the universal *umma*, in terms of the relationships that tie Muslim communities together, their rights and obligations in the lands of Islam and in foreign lands.

Islam seems always to have had a pragmatic approach to these questions and no clear-cut dogma was worked out. This is understandable, since the ideal of Muslims has always been to live under Muslim government, and Muslim political theory provides comprehensive rules for the functioning of such government. If religious political theory were to lay rules for contingencies outside the realm of the Muslim state, it would thereby have implicitly sanctioned such situations.

An undefinable feeling of expectation and a vague hope were everpresent in the midst of Muslims in China, that someday, somehow, somebody might come and restore them to *dār al-islām* and to full participation in the life of the universal *umma*. This was something like the mystique of "next year in Jerusalem" which has always been present among the Jews in the Diaspora, or like the millenarian expectations among Chinese sectarian movements. Not unlike these two groups, Chinese Muslims, while entertaining their deeply ingrained aspirations, went about their daily business wholeheartedly. At the same time, due to the options that were theoretically open to them, they devoted considerable time and attention in educating and preparing themselves for such contingencies.

To this end, the Muslim community consistently underwent indoctrination on various levels. First, the Muslims kept from becoming Chinese; they reinforced their sense of superiority and distinctiveness, and encouraged the Muslim to remain socially and economically as independant of the Chinese as possible. Second, the Muslims became better members of their community through strong communal organization, inculcation of Islamic values, communal worship and activities, a total and unqualified identification with their fellow Muslims in the congregation, and moral submission to the authority of the Imam. Third, the Chinese Muslim was made a conscious member of the world Muslim community. This was achieved, as we have seen, by cultivating in the Muslim the centrality of Arabia, Islam, the Islamic Empire, and Islamic traditions and values. But this was not all.

The daily prayers in the mosque were not only a communal worship, but also a way of identifying with all Muslims who faced the same direction of prayer (*qibla*)—Holy Mecca, the place of inception of Islam and conception of the Prophet. Some Chinese Muslims who could afford it went on the *ḥajj* (pilgrimage), and participated with the Muslim multitudes in common rituals that must have generated a feeling of religious exaltation. On the way to and from Mecca, some Chinese Muslim notables (*ʿulamāʾ*) visited Islamic centers such as Cairo and Constantinople, and on their return home they told their fellow Muslims of the marvels of the Islamic world and of their brethren there.

Muslims from Persia, India and Turkey seem to have paid sporadic visits to Muslim communities in China. Some of them, especially scholars, stayed for long periods of time and presumably shared their knowledge with their coreligionists. Chinese Muslims also met other Muslims in Asia on their way to the *ḥajj*. They received hospitality in mosques in Colombo, in Singapore and Hanoi. From Yunnan, Chinese Muslims maintained a permanent correspondence with Muslim scholars in Arabia and southeast Asia, whence they sought advice when they faced problems of interpretation of the *sharīʿa*.

Material Versus Value-System Acculturation

The picture of Chinese Islam depicted above can at best reflect the broad lines of the main stream of Muslims in China, but is by no means applicable to every Muslim in every Muslim community throughout the empire. For there remain ambiguities, uncertainties, paradoxes and puzzles that defy definition, generalization and analysis. For example, Chinese Muslims were described as trying to avoid contact with the Chinese and to focus their activities, economic and social, within their communities. Yet, many Muslims not only took part in the Chinese system but became prominent in it, especially (though not exclusively) in the military domain. Examples abound: Zheng He, the famous maritime explorer of the Ming, who preceded Columbus by over a century, was Muslim. Many high ranking Muslim officials climbed through the examination system to obtain high-ranking posts in Chinese government, as did Ma Xinyi, Governor General of Fujian and Zhejiang in the late Qing.

This ambivalent attitude can be explained in terms of the pragmatic approach of Islam to the necessities of life, because Chinese Muslims did not, indeed could not, isolate themselves from a society on which they depended in many respects. But it is also possible to imagine that Muslim inroads into the highest positions of power in the government, especially in the military, (which was the paradigm of power) may be attributed to a sublimation of their frustrations. They could thereby show to the Chinese who despised them that they too could make it to the top, despite their underprivileged position. Moreover, Muslims in top positions may have been thought able to intervene from within the system on behalf of their coreligionists, and that in itself justified their deed, since in the final analysis they helped protect and preserve Islam rather than turning their backs on it. The Holy Qurʾān justifies such a measure: ''Good deeds exonerate evil doings.''

The record shows that in China many Muslim communities and Muslim individuals have drifted away from their heritage and acculturated more fully to the host culture than the main stream of Chinese Islam, especially in isolated places where maintaining one's distinctiveness could become a matter of daily embarrassment and constant nuisance rather than a source of pride and superiority. So we hear of Muslims who practiced ancestor worship and local spirit worship, of Muslims who adopted Chinese mourning practices, and even of Chinese who respect some tenets of Islam but are unaware of their Islamic origin. There are missionary accounts of Muslims who would gather to listen to Christian preaching and find similarities between their faith and Christianity, a thing unheard of in lands of Islam.

These phenomena are due to the organizational fragmentation of Chinese Islam and the absence of supra-communal authority that could look after the needs of small and isolated communities and save them from extinction. For, as Skinner has remarked, ''The greater number of individuals who carry a species or a culture, the greater its chances of survival.'' Local compromises that Islam had made during its expansion, and the incorporation of *ʿurf* (local custom) into the *sharīʿa*, had brought about the spread of the faith. But that was achieved under a victorious conquering Islam, whose self-confidence allowed it to compromise. It was a compromise by a condescending collective, sure of itself and its ultimate victory, using accomodation and compromise as a tactic to get to an end. In China, the Muslims who compromised with certain Chinese customs were at best tolerated, in a land where they were disliked, exposed to ridicule and to repeated onslaughts by their hosts. Their compromise, which centered almost exclusively on adoption of Chinese material culture, rather than acculturation into the Confucian value system, manifested the unbridgeability of the gap which separated Islam from the Chinese system.

This compromise, far from plastering over the incompatibilities between these two self-confident cultures, on the contrary exposed the built-in limitations of each of them to come halfway to meet the other. Therefore, Muslim dormant aspirations, which are inherent in the Islamic system of belief, erupted into a full scale confrontation with the Confucian state, when coexistence was no longer feasible under the Qing Dynasty.

The fact that the rebellions of the nineteenth century were suppressed did not lead to the submission of the Muslims, nor did the latter ever reconcile thereafter with the idea of a sizable Muslim population ruled by the Chinese host culture. The Chinese, under the Republic, made tremendous efforts to appease the Muslims by recognizing them as one of the "five peoples of China." Sun Yat-sen himself became devoted to this aim, because he was aware of the numerical and political weight of the world Muslim community, of which Chinese Muslims considered themselves part and parcel. The problem, however, was not one of compromise, because both the Islamic and the Chinese political traditions are such as to leave no room for an accommodation. The Chinese state has always been, and still remains, unitarian and shuns the idea of a multistate federation, an idea which was accepted, at least in theory, by the Soviet Union. The Muslim ideology requires assumption of political power, as the will of Allah has to be implemented on earth by a political system; therefore, no Muslim would find his identity within a non-Muslim unitarian state. No wonder then, that even under communist rule, outbursts of Muslim particularism erupted, when the lax period of the "Hundred Flowers" gave Muslims the opportunity to express themselves. They discredited the "Fatherland" concept of the regime and flatly declared that "China is not the fatherland of the Hui Nationality ... Arabic is the language of the Hui people.... All the Hui people of the world belong to one family..."[15]

In modern China, these problems are further compounded by new considerations that derive from novel circumstances. First, unlike other minority groups, such as the Mongols, the Tibetans and the Zhuang, the Muslims are not attached to any particular territory, although they admittedly constitute a majority in areas such as Ningxia and Xinjiang, or a very sizable minority such as in Gangu and Yunnan. They can be found everywhere throughout the country, and every large city is likely to have its Hui section. Second, unlike other minority groups in China, whose home base may be included *in toto* within the confines of the People's Republic (e.g., Tibet), the Muslims, whose focus of identity remains with the universal *umma* of Islam, regard themselves as a Chinese branch of an alien culture, not a minority guest culture in China. The daily validation of their membership in the universal *umma* is at the basis of Muslim ritual, and one of the "Pillars of Islam" is the tenet of *ḥajj*, the pilgrimage to Mecca—the Holy Place of all Muslims.

Third, despite Chinese attempts to differentiate within the Muslim Community in China between the Hui of China proper, the Uighurs of Xinjiang, and the other Turkic minorities of central Asia—Uzbek, Kirghiz and Kazakh—a general sentiment of Islamic brotherhood unites, potentially if not practically, all those splinters into one living social and cultural group, which given certain circumstances, may seek political expression as well. As long as the *divide et impera* policy of the Chinese state prevails, however the ethnic, and linguistic differences between the Hui and the other Muslim groups in China may be cultivated. Thus, when reference is made in state announcements to the population of Xinjiang, the purpose would seem to serve the policy of emphasizing parochial peculiarities and to stem the rise of Muslim unity throughout the land. Fourth, Islam is not only a culture but also a totalistic way of life, which inseparably encompasses politics and religion, and irrevocably strives to bring to bear the Islamic political theory; this carries with it the seeds of Muslim statehood. When a Muslim minority happens to live in a non-Muslim state, it remains in many ways outside that polity and nurtures separatistic ideals. Fifth, more recently, because of the mounting power and wealth of some Islamic countries, Islam has become a success story, something to be proud of. Moreover, the new institution of the "Islamic Conferences," which has been convening yearly since 1969, has given a new Impetus to popular, if not political, Pan-Islamic sentiments. One may conjecture that in the post-"Gang of Four" era, as China seems to be less rigid toward the outside world, Chinese Islam may be affected by these Pan-Islamic currents, and consequently by separatistic trends, as has been the case with other Muslim minorities in Asia (the Philippines, Thailand, and Burma).

Conclusion

Are Muslims who live in China "Muslims in China" or "Chinese Muslims?" They certainly were both, at one time or another, and they have even attempted to go out of China while remaining there, by seceding from the empire. So, it appears that as no large-scale process of Islamization of Confucianism has been possible in China, so no intensive and far-reaching Sinicization of Islam has been feasible. The confrontation has been between two very self-confident cultures, both having a long history of swallowing others rather than being swallowed up. Their mutual inability to overwhelm each other, which was underlined by occasional outbursts of confrontation between them, persisted even when they encountered each other on a majority/minority basis. This is due, of course, to the potent sense of belonging to the universal *umma*, whose basis of power and center of creativity, being outside China, kept feeding the inner strength of the Muslim Chinese community and its sense of self-confidence.

Paradoxically, only as long as Sinicization was not pressed by the Chinese rulers would this process go on unhindered, and more and more Muslims on the margins would fall off to Confucianism. But when Sinicization was forced or Islam oppressed, the main body of Muslims would rise up, shrug off the outer signs of material acculturation, forget the niceties of good neighborhood with the Chinese, and raise the banner of a separate identity. This seems to have been the case not only in Imperial China, but in the contemporary situation as well.[16]

NOTES

1 L. V. Sodestrom, "The Mohammedan Women of China," *Moslem World* 4 (1914): 79-80.

2 Marco Polo, *The Book of Ser Marco Polo, the Venetian, Concerning the Kingdoms and Marvels of the East*, trans. and ed. with notes, Henry Yule (London: J. Murray, 1871), p. 153. See also my "Islamization and Sinicization in Chinese Islam," in Nehemiah Levtzion, ed., *Conversion to Islam* (New York and London: Holmes & Meier, 1979), pp. 166ff.

3 Ibn Baṭṭūṭa, *Voyages d'Ibn Batoutah*, trans. B. R. Sanguinetti and C. Defrémery [text in Arabic and French] (Paris: Imprimerie Nationale, 1922), vol. 4, p. 285.

4 Owen Lattimore, *The Desert Road to Turkestan* (London: Methuen, 1928), pp. 165-66.

5 See Marshall Broomhall, *Islam in China: A Neglected Problem* (London: Morgan and Scott, 1910), p. 244.

6 Lattimore, *Desert Road*, p. 184.

7 Broomhall, *Islam in China*, pp. 244-45.

8 Lattimore, *Desert Road*, p. 202.

9 Lattimore, p. 203.

10 Broomhall, pp. 224-25.

11 J. Levenson, "The Province, the Nation and the World: The Problem of Chinese Identity," in J. Levenson, ed., *Modern China, an Interpretive Anthology* (New York: Macmillan, 1970), pp. 287-88.

12 Morrison, *An Embassy to Peking in 1816*, cited by Broomhall, p. 166.

13 Lattimore, p. 56. "Rum" was probably Constantinople.

14 Arnold J. Vissière, *Etudes Sino-Mahometanes* (Paris: E. Leroux, p. 120.

15 *New China News Agency*, Jan. 16, 1958.

16 See my "Islamization and Sinicization in Chinese Islam," (ref. above note 2). I have dealt with some of these same aspects of Islam in China elsewhere; see esp. "The Muslim Minority in Traditional China," *Asian and African Studies* 10/2 (1975): 101-26, and "Established Islam and Marginal Islam in China: From Eclecticism to Syncretism," *Journal of the Economic and Social History of the Orient* 21/1 (1978).

Contributions to Asian Studies, Vol. XVII

The Qurʾān in China*

JIN YIJIU
Institute for Research on World Religions, Beijing, Peoples Republic of China

TWENTY-NINE YEARS after the Hijra an envoy was sent out by ʿUthmān, the third Caliph of Islam (reg. A.D. 644-656). The envoy presented tributes to the imperial court, to establish friendly relations with China. The year in which this is said to have taken place (A.D. 651), which coincides with the second year of Yonghui of the Tang Dynasty, has been regarded as the beginning of the propagation of Islam in China. This was first assumed by the late Professor Chen Yuan in his treatise entitled *An Outline History of the Propagation of Islam in China*, and has been generally accepted by Chinese scholars, although there are different opinions as to details. With the spread of Islam, the Qurʾān as its holy scripture was also introduced into China.

Historical Background

In the mid-seventh century, Persian and Arab Muslim merchants came to China successively both by sea and by land, to settle and trade in Changan (now Xian), and the coastal cities such as Guangzhou (Canton), quanzhou (Zayton, as it was called by Marco Polo), and Hangzhou (Hangchow). These early travelers were treated as *Fanke* (foreign merchants) among whom Islam prevailed.

The earliest Chinese account of Islam is Du Huan's *Jingxingji* [Recollections of the Journey]. Du had been taken captive while joining the expedition westward led by Gao Xianzhi (d. A.D. 755), and had lived in Arab lands under Arab hegemony for eleven years, from 751 to 762. When he returned to China, he wrote his *Recollections* giving an account of Islam as he had witnessed it there. The book, though no longer extant, was quoted by his uncle Du You (735-812) in *Tongdian* [General Records]. Unfortunately the above-mentioned account does not give us much information about Islam in China at the early period in which it was written.

From the time when Islam was first introduced until the Song Dynasty (Northern Song, 960-1126), the Chinese scholars and non-Muslims knew very little about the Islamic faith or rituals, and often interpreted this religion from

* This paper is a translation by the author, with minor assistance on matters of English style by the editor, of an article which first appeared in "'Gulanjing' zai Zhongguo," in *Shijie zongjiao yanjiu* 1/3 (1981 Beijing): 128-32. Professor Jin presented an English version of the paper at the International Association of the History of Religions in Winnipeg, Canada in August 1980.

the Buddhist point of view. In *Xinshi* [Record of the Heart] by Zheng Suonan of the Song Dynasty, we read: "The Huihui worship the Buddha and have built a tall tower ... from which they call the Buddha aloud continuously," and in *Nanhai baiyong* [Hundred Poems from the South Sea] by Fang Xinru it says, "The foreign tower built during the Tang Dynasty is called *Huaisheng ta* [The Tower in Memory of the Saint].... The foreigners climb to the top at dawn to call the name of the Buddha." The "Buddha" here refers to Allah whom the Muslims worship, the tower is the minaret of the mosque, and the calling is the *adhān* practiced by the muezzin [*muʾadhdhin*] to summon the Muslims to prayer. In *Lingwai daida* [Substitute for Answers from over the Mountains] by Zhou Qufei it says "in Mecca, where the Buddha Muhammad passed away, there is an abbey where the Buddha lived, surrounded by walls and houses made of colorful jade. At the anniversaries of the death of the Buddha, kings of various *Dashi* (Arab) countries sent messengers who brought silver, gold and valuables for alms (*zakāt*) and silk to cover the abbey." In Zhao Rugua's *Zhufan shi* [Records of Various Countries] it tells more or less the same thing: "Both the king and the people of *Dashi* worship Heaven. There was a Buddha named Mahamo." "A tomb is built in the place where the Buddha lived." "Mahamo" is the expression in the southern dialect for Muhammad and the abbey means the Kaʿba in Mecca. Although from the point of view of orthodox Muslims it's an obvious mistake to call Muhammad "the founder of Islam," much less the "Buddha," they were following the example of the Buddhists, who called their founder, Sakyamuni, "The Buddha."

Persian, Arab and Central Asian Muslims began to immigrate into China in increasing numbers from the thirteenth century, especially at the beginning of the Yuan Dynasty (Mongols, 1271-1368), when they scattered all over the country. By mingling and intermarrying with the Hans, Uighurs and Mongolians, the immigrants gradually formed a new nationality—the Hui. In the meantime, Islam was spreading throughout China. Nevertheless, so far as we know the Qurʾān had not yet been mentioned by its proper name though it had been alluded to in such phrases in Chinese literature or in the epigraphs of mosques as "the scripture is all in a foreign language," and "the Muslims are absorbed in reciting the scripture," and "to recite the scripture and observe the fast," etc. Up to the Ming Dynasty (1368-1644), Huang Xingzeng's *Xiyang chaogong dianlu* [Records of the Tributes paid by the Western Countries] still could say that "In the Tianfang (Arab) Kingdom ... people make the Buddha images out of gold." Both in Mao Yuanyi's *Wubizhi* [Records of Military Classics] and Luo Yuejiong's *Xianbin lu* [Records of Neighbouring Lands], the Qurʾān is called "the Buddhist scripture" and it is further stated that "there are thirty collections of Buddhist scripture in their country." It was only as late as the Qing Dynasty (Manchus, 1645-1911), that the name "Qurʾān" was transliterated into various forms of pronunciation in Chinese literature, such as *Runʾerhan* in *Xiyu jianwenlu* [Records of Experiences in Xiyu] and *Kuruan* in the *Xiyu shuidaoji* [Records of Rivers in Xiyu]. The transliteration "*Gulan*" by Islamic scholars is nearest to its original pronunciation.

These remarks indicate the erroneous conception of Islam held by Chinese scholars in those days, and we can well imagine that their ignorance of Islam was chiefly due to the fact that Islam had been propagated in China only among the foreign Muslim merchants at first, and later only among the Hui and but a few other nationalities in China. Moreover, it had neither an organization nor missionaries to carry on its propagation in the same way that Islam had spread elsewhere.

The Qurʾān in the Earlier Periods

In their contacts with the Hans, Uighurs and the Mongolians, the Persian, Arab and Central Asian Muslims who immigrated to China used the Han language as a means of communication, and Han became their mother tongue after they became established as the Hui nationality. In their religious rituals, however, the Hui still retained the use of Arabic. So most Muslims went to the mosque in childhood to learn Arabic from the *akhund* (religious leader) so as to be able to recite the Qurʾān. Some learned Arabic through the Persian language. After learning the Qurʾān for a long time, many Muslims were able to commit the familiar passages to memory, though without understanding much, if anything, of the meaning. Because it is not an easy thing to learn Arabic under such "indirect" circumstances, even some *akhund*s merely knew the general idea, without knowing the profound meaning. Akhund Yang Zhongming has written that "the true significance of the [Muslim] scripture has been expounded only orally in our country. Although at the beginning the preaching was conveyed implicitly (after all, the spoken words remained superficial) and error led to error, so in the long run it became unintelligible." Such traditional methods of passing on the scripture orally and committing it to memory continued until the 1920s.

Although the Qurʾān has always and everywhere been transmitted orally, the case of China is interesting because unlike in the rest of the Abode of Islam, Muslims in China did not have a concomitant literary transmission of the Qurʾān. Yet for all that, the Qurʾān survived and retained a place of importance.

Hu Puzhao (1522-1597) first established the system of monastic education to train *akhund*s for mosques. His schools provided systematic teaching and lectures on the scripture. The students, called *manla*s or caliphs, finished numerous mandatory courses (some said this included thirteen volumes on the scriptures) prior to their graduation. There was no printed edition of the Qurʾān at that time. The students had to copy the scripture by hand and to learn the script while copying it. Those students who wished to pursue advanced studies had to travel far, loaded with baggage that included pens and paper, to visit well-known scholars for instruction. Thus, the Prophet's well-known Hadith, "seek knowledge, even in China," had some meaning even in China. In this manner over a long period of time the Chinese Muslims developed particular styles of calligraphy in copying the Qurʾān.

Three styles of calligraphy were mentioned in *Qingjing siji* [Notes about the *Qingjing* Mosque] by Wu Jian of the Yuan Dynasty, namely, the seal character, the regular script and the cursive hand. Many such handwritten copies are preserved in mosques, as well as in museums, as historical relics. One of these, a copy dated 1318, has been kept in the Dongsi Mosque in Beijing and is valued both by Muslims and by other Chinese scholars. The scripture was also copied on parchments or engraved on bones of cattle, and today these are regarded as precious cultural relics in the Xinjiang area.

Cherished copies of the Qurʾān owned by Muslim families were mostly bought at high prices during their pilgrimages to Mecca, and were regarded as the most valuable gifts at consequent weddings in China. And it was not uncommon to find Muslims in the northwest carrying a piece of paper or cloth with the scripture written on it as an amulet or otherwise as an evidence of atonement.

The Chinese Muslims also attach great importance to the recitation of the Qurʾān. They are divided into the high-pitched sect and the low-pitched sect as a result of difference in tone and style of recitation.

In the first year (1862) of Tongzhi in the Qing Dynasty, Du Wenxiu (1823-1872) of Yunnan sponsored the first engraving and printing of the Qurʾān in China. The publication helped to bring about the popularization of the Qurʾān among Muslims throughout the country.

The passages of scripture used during the *ṣalāt* (congregational prayers) were arranged by the Imams and Muslim scholars in various selections for different religious occasions, such as *Shiba duan* [Eighteen Passages] and *Heting* [Selections]. The *Heting* consists of one- and three-volume editions, among which the 1875 edition and *Heting quanji* [The Complete Selections] were the most popular in the nineteenth century. Some selections are prefaced by an introduction in Chinese. Such selections facilitate learning the Qurʾān in Arabic.

Qurʾān Transliteration and Translation

For centuries no Chinese translation of the Qurʾān existed. One reason was the lack of translators among the Muslims. Another was that the Muslims considered it too difficult to convey the true meaning of the sacred book, which Allah had revealed in Arabic, into languages other than the original one, and they believed that it would be blasphemy to render it improperly. This, of course, caused great inconvenience to the Muslims who wished to grasp the real meaning of the scripture. With the spread of Islam, more and more Muslims wanted the scripture to be explained in Chinese. So, while most of the Imams and *akhund*s were devoted to the traditional forms of education described above, some scholars eventually made the attempt to translate the Qurʾān into Chinese, and efforts to do so have increased in recent times.

In China, the history of translating the Qurʾān may be roughly divided into three periods. The first is the period of "extract translations," during which the translators combined the activity of translation with their own writing and commentary based on the Qurʾān. The most important scholars were Wang Daiyu (1570-1660), Ma Zhu (1640-1711) and Liu Zhi (1660-1730), who were generally acknowledged by Muslims as "masters of the four religions" (i.e. Buddhism, Taoism, Confucianism and Islam), or "most prolific writers with a good command of both Chinese and Arabic" as well as "learned scholars proficient in Confucianism."

Wang Daiyu says in *Zhengjiao zhenquan* [True Explanation of the Correct Religion] that the forty chapters therein are "extract" translations done in the course of several years, in which "the ideas all come from the Holy Scripture [Qurʾān]." Of course, the book is in no sense a translation of the Qurʾān, but as its ideas are based on the Qurʾān, it has been generally well received and respected by the Chinese Muslims, and is even regarded as a book of golden rule and precious precept. Ma Zhu says in *Jinjing shu* [A Memorial to the Throne for Presenting the Scripture] that he "compiled the scripture of the true religion, and translated its main points" so as to present it for perusal to Emperor Kangxi (1662-1723) of the Qing Dynasty. Though he declared that he was absolutely faithful to the original text in his extract translation, and that he dared not to "use false words to betray his Lord," nor dared he to "use false words to curry favor with the emperor," still, his book, like that of Wang Daiyu's, is not a translation of the Qurʾān either. It is the same with Liu Zhi, who quoted and rendered freely excerpts from the Qurʾān in his books without making a close translation. In his own words, what he had done was just "to convey the meaning."

Though the above-mentioned books can hardly be counted as translations of the Qurʾān in a strict sense, and their wording is somewhat permeated with terms and concepts of Confucianism, and their publication hasn't been of much practical significance in the religious life of the Muslims, nevertheless, they mark the beginning of the Chinese translation of the Qurʾān and have helped, more or less, the Muslims to understand the scripture and the doctrine through the Chinese text in those books. Later, the translation movement entered a second stage.

The period of translating selections from the Qurʾān began from the latter half of the eighteenth century and lasted to the beginning of the twentieth. These translations of selections were made to meet practical needs. There were two kinds of translations at the time. One was the transliteration of the selections, i.e. the transliteration of the Arabic scripture into Chinese characters, forming a book of Arabic with the reproduction in Chinese of the Arabic pronunciation, so that the Chinese Muslims could recite without a teacher. Under this category there are the *Hanli heting* of 1882 [Selections from the Qurʾān Transliterated into Chinese Characters] and *Heting zhenjing* [Selections from the True Qurʾān]. Another kind was in the form of commentary, i.e. the transliteration was supplemented with translation and commentary, such as *Jing Han zhujie heting* of 1866, also entitled *Zhujie heting* [Selections from the Qurʾān, in Arabic and Chinese, with Commentary], Ma Kuilin and Yang Deyuan's *Baoming zhenjing*, 1919 [Selections from the Precious Qurʾān] and Li

Tingxiang's *Tienjing yijie*, 1924 [A Paraphrase of the Qurʾān]. Although these books sought primarily to reproduce Arabic pronunciation with Chinese characters, it happens nonetheless that there are a lot of monastic terms associated with other Chinese classics or suggested by the Chinese transliteration of Arabic terms, and this has affected the meaning in the later translations to a certain degree.

The third period, of attempting whole translations of the Qurʾān, began from the 1920s. As a matter of fact, as early as in the Qing Dynasty, Ma Fuchu (1794-1894) already started such a translation while he was engaged in writing other books. The work had been carried on for twenty volumes then left unfinished. And, of the twenty volumes, only five were saved from fire, and later, it is said, these five volumes were published under the title of *Baoming zhenjing zhijie* [A Direct Translation of the Precious Qurʾān].

The earliest translation of the whole of the Qurʾān is Li Tiezheng's *Kelanjing* [The Qurʾān], published in Beijing, in 1927; it was translated from Kamoto Ken'ichi's Japanese version with reference to Rodwell's English version. It is the first complete Chinese version of the Qurʾān though not translated from the Arabic original. Later, Ji Juemi's *Hanyi Gulanjing* [The Qurʾān in Chinese], published in Shanghai in 1931, was actually translated by Akhund Li Yuchen, Xue Ziming and Fan Kangfu. The project started in 1928 and was finished in 1931. They also consulted the Japanese and English versions. Both books were neglected by the Muslims, however, for they regarded them with suspicion because they were translations done by non-Muslims.

While Ji's translation was going on, the Imams also began their translation of the Qurʾān. The first one to come out in Beiping (now Beijing) in 1932 was Akhund Wang Wenqing or Wang Jingzhai's *Gulanjing yijie* [A Translation of the Qurʾān with Commentary]. This was the first Chinese version of the Qurʾān done by a Muslim. Later, there was Akhund Liu Jinbiao's *Kelan Hanyi fuzhuan* [The Qurʾān in Chinese Translation with Commentary], published in Beiping in 1943, then again the second edition of Wang Jingzhai's translation, published in Shanghai in 1946 and Akhund Yang Zhongming's *Gulanjing dayi* [Cardinal Principles of the Qurʾān] published in Beiping in 1947. Several more manuscripts of translations are either unfinished or yet unpublished.

The language used in the above-mentioned books is quite obscure, and, with the "monastic" terms suggestive of non-Muslim ideas intermingled therein, these translations are often quite difficult to understand, and some of the translations are really only summaries, so the reader can hardly get a whole or an accurate impression of the scripture if he or she must rely solely upon them. Shi Zizhou's *Gulanjing guoyu yijie* [The Qurʾān in Standard Chinese Translation with Commentary], published in 1958, was translated from the English version, and was checked by Imams Ding Zhongming, Xiong Zhenzong and Chang Zixuan against the Arabic text. It does not read smoothly, though it has the advantage of being in the style of the spoken language.

Another Chinese version of the Qurʾān, translated directly from the Arabic, was finished by the well-known scholar Ma Jian, the late professor of

Beijing University, during the War of Resistance against Japan. Part of the translation was published in eight volumes in 1952, with some revisions made later. The Chinese Social Sciences Publishing House published the entire translation in 1981.

With the publication of the Chinese version of the Qur᾽ān, research on the Qur᾽ān has also begun in China. Courses on the Qur᾽ān are now taught in some colleges in China to introduce students to the content and principle ideas of Muslim scripture.

Contributions to Asian Studies, Vol. XVII

Ritual and Symbolic Aspects of Islam in African Contexts

AZIM NANJI
Oklahoma State University, Stillwater, Oklahoma, U.S.A.

THIS ESSAY EXAMINES two African Muslim groups. The material for the first group, a Muslim village community in Guinea, is derived exclusively from a literary source, *L'Enfant Noir* by the well-known West African novelist, Camara Laye.[1] For the second group, the Nizārī Ismāᶜīlīs of East Africa, the source material for the analysis of a key ritual is drawn from their recorded literary tradition known as the *ginān*s as well as field studies on the group done in India, Pakistan and East Africa.[2]

L'Enfant Noir, a somewhat idealized and fictional autobiography illustrates from the vantage point of a growing boy acting both as informant and interpreter, various episodes showing the integration of Muslim practices and values within a local context and indicating patterns of life and activity that are informed by Islam and yet giving wider meaning to social and cultural values rooted in indigenous traditions of the area. The Nizārī Ismāᶜīlīs on the other hand, are a migrant group originating in the Subcontinent, who have made the East African countries of Kenya, Uganda and Tanzania their home since the turn of this century.

With regard to the study of the Islamic presence in sub-Saharan Africa it can be remarked that the work is still in its early stages of development. Though a variety of monographs and specialized studies are now available, the larger methodological issues have yet to be examined in any detail. One major tendency that has marked some of the more general studies, relates to the problem of "syncretism" in African Islam. Applying notions developed by earlier Islamicists on unity and diversity within Islam, some of these works have made the assumption that because sub-Saharan Islam reveals a layer of "classical, normative" Islam juxtaposed with an indigenized tradition of Muslim practice and piety, that such forms of religious life can be labelled as "popular" Islam.[3] Clifford Geertz in his now widely recognized classic, *Islam Observed* notes that, "religious faith, even when it is fed from a common source, is as much a particularizing force as a generalizing one and indeed whatever universality a given religious tradition manages to attain arises from its ability to engage a widening set of individual, even idiosyncratic, conceptions of life and yet somehow sustain and elaborate them all."[4] It is noteworthy that this insight, expected among those engaged in the study of Islam from humanistic perspectives, arises out of the study of cultural anthropology. Historical and literary perspectives on Islam in Africa have tended to assume a classical period or intent within Muslim history and tradition, and then go on to regard developments in local contexts as representing a departure, or in a negative sense an "accommodation." Though this legalistic or fundamentalist position may be tenable in its own terms, it has led to a neglect of interesting manifestations of the Islamic presence interacting with African traditions.

The wider academic debate in religious studies regarding "popular" or "local" religion reveals a need to move away from a discussion of terms to an attempt to present a perspective based on analysis of the observed or studied experience. Rather than concerning themselves with issues raised by the designation of religious life within a specific local context as "popular" (as against "*savant*") or unofficial (as against "official" or "ecclesiastical") a number of scholars of so-called "popular" religion are beginning to address themselves to religious life in local contexts in terms of the experience and response revealed by the presence of a particular religion in that area.[5]

Having drawn earlier from the experiences of a cultural anthropologist of Islam, one may add to that perspective a lesson from the study of Muslim architecture. The "vocabulary" and the "language" of Muslim architecture varies from region to region. Yet it can be argued that it is possible to identify a spirit that informs these diverse creations which is inspired by a sensitivity and awareness that seeks to adapt Islamic values to local conditions. What gives various regional architectural forms a sense of unity, is the perception and commitment to symbols derived from Islam, which then in their expression reflect an architectural vernacular rooted in the regions in which they emerge and develop.[6]

By using a combination of literary and other approaches based on field work, it is hoped that the study of African Islam can better address itself to significant questions of religious change and of how such materials illustrate the attempt of peoples converted to Islam to bring their existing world views to bear on new social conditions and patterns of belief. Another merit of literary sources is that besides social factors, they also integrate emotional and psychological factors into their perspective, showing responses at the level of individual as well as communal life. They also provide a means of directing attention more on the meaning of ritual for the people involved and less on the merely functional problems related to religious practice and experience.

L'Enfant Noir

This portrayal of a child's emergence into adulthood amidst the changing world of Guinean life in West Africa refers to several events that reveal a pattern of Muslim life woven into the context of traditional African culture. For this particular study, I have chosen to highlight some key symbols and two significant episodes to illustrate this pattern.

There are several religious symbols and learning experiences that reflect the initial stages of the child's upbringing. The first is the snake, considered the eternal guiding spirit of the people, the symbol of interdependence between the material and the spiritual world and of the transmission of knowledge from the world of spirits to the world of persons. The second is the Qurʾān school where the children receive their early schooling and develop a sensitivity for the recited or spoken "word," the tool for expression of knowledge in an oral culture. Equating intelligence and learning with the spoken word, Laye states, "if intelligence seemed slower it was because reflection preceded speech and because speech itself was an important matter."[7] The Qurʾān as the revealed and spoken word of God thus enters into the child's consciousness as embodying three aspects of traditional wisdom and learning—reflection, speech and intelligence. The verbal meaning of the revealed word cannot be separated from the behavior it engenders.

Such a concept of traditional learning as reflected in actual practice is traced in a description that Laye gives of his father's work as a goldsmith. This memorable episode takes on the significance of a religious ritual reenacting the cosmic event of Creation. There is an insistence on the idea of harmony and beauty that emerge out of the smelting and the chaos, echoing many a Qurʾānic verse. The ritualistic aspect of the episode is emphasized in the incantations and chanting that accompany the forging of the gold in ornament, the spiritual world participating with human hands in the process of transformation. The praise-singer composes his most powerful songs at this moment, the transformation impelling him to greater creativity while the gold is moulded into beautiful patterns. It is also significant that the craftsman working with gold must purify himself through ablutions and abstain from sex during the whole time of what is described as a "ceremony." After the completion of the work and the general offering of good wishes and congratulations, the craftsman makes an offering to all present of cola nuts, the token of courtesy, good will and solidarity.

A different type of transformation is traced in the events that mark the boy's initiation into adulthood. Among Muslims, the act of circumcision generally follows soon after birth or when the boy is fairly young. As described in Guinean Muslim society, this act is postponed until just before the boy is ready to undertake the responsibilities of adult life. The circumcision is, however, preceded by a preliminary initatory act associated with *Konden Diara*, a frightening mythical presence with whom the initiates must come to terms. During this ceremony, boys join the society of the uninitiated comprising all the uncircumcized youth of twelve, thirteen and fourteen years of age. The event takes place on the night before the feast marking the end of the month of Ramaḍān, ending the Muslim month of fasting. Among the Muslims of Guinea it is called the "ceremony of lions," because the boys spend a night on the outside in a sacred spot, surrounded by the terrifying roars that appear to be those of lions, the event is described as a "test, a training in hardship, a rite...."[8] The elements inherent in the ceremony, which are of course of great symbolic import as well, are remarkable for their juxtaposition of the ritual of initiation and the ritual of fasting during Ramaḍān, both involving notions of testing, of discipline, of community solidarity and above all of strengthening the capability of the human will for the responsibilities, fears and traumas of adult and community life. The initiation ceremony reaches a climax the next day in the feasting that follows Ramaḍān, marking an end to the period of trial and evoking a sense of celebration and even triumph.

Later on comes the actual circumcision ceremony. In its various phases, it follows a pattern common to several African societies: the public ceremonies of communal dancing and feasting and the private ceremonies involving the separation and sequestering of those to be circumcized in a hut. Finally after the actual operation, there follows a period of healing accompanied by secret instruction and training for adult life. In summing up the impact of the event, the author refers to the alternating rhythms of joy and gravity and observes that all was overshadowed by the fact that the "event which is commemorated was the most important event in life: to be exact, the beginning of new life.... Life itself would spring from the shedding of our blood."[9]

This new beginning prepares the youths through "secret" knowledge which has revealed to them a code of conduct and conferred on them capabilities for undertaking adult responsibilities; it also means that they now have a commitment to the religious and social organizations that support the group. The intermingling of Islamic symbols, such as the feast of Ramaḍān, the role of the teacher (or "Shaykh" to use the Sufi term), in the initiation and circumcision rituals, represent one illustration of how Muslim and Guinean world views are fused in the cultural milieu and provide a broader frame of reference within which the young African Muslim responds and acts.

The Nizārī Ismāʿīlī Ceremony of *Ghaṭ-Pāṭ*

The traditional literature called the *ginān*s, which has been preserved among this group over several centuries, makes reference to certain rituals that became established in the community after its conversion to Islam. The process of conversion which took place in the Subcontinent from the thirteenth century onwards was carried out by Ismāʿīlī *dāʿī*s [missionaries], known in the community as *pīr*s. One of the rituals that became established was a ceremony called *ghaṭ-pāṭ*.[10] As described in the ancient literature, those who had converted from Hinduism into Islam participated in a group ritual where they drank a sip of sacred water after having given up the *janōi* (*jane'ū*), a sacred thread worn by Hindus. When some of the Nizārī Ismāʿīlīs migrated to East Africa during the nineteenth and twentieth centuries, they established *jamāʿāt-khānas*[11] in the new centers of settlement. These *jamāʿāt-khānas* functioned as a house of assembly and prayers, much the same as they had among both Ismāʿīlis and Sufis in the Subcontinent. Though several specifically Indo-Muslim aspects of the community's life became altered in the new land, the ritual of *ghaṭ-pāṭ* continued to play an important part in their religious life centered on the *jamāʿāt-khāna*.

The term *ghaṭ-pāṭ* is a compound derived from two Sanskrit words, *ghaṭ* (a vessel for water) and *pāṭa* (a low, long dais-like table on which the vessels are placed). Within the community, the ceremony is also referred to in Persian as *Āb-i-shifā*ʾ ("water of healing").[12]

The water placed in the vessel was generally mixed with that obtained from the well of *zamzam* or with small clay tablets from Shīʿite holy places such as Karbala. Special prayers may also have been said over the water by the Imam during a visit to the community. In this way the sacred character of the water is established. The vessels used during the ceremony are also cleansed ritually through recitation of prayer and use of incense. Within the community, a link is established between this ceremony and the practice of the Prophet Muhammad, who is said to have performed initiatory rites for the early converts to Islam. Parallel traditions of course also existed among many Sufi groups in the Subcontinent and elsewhere in the Muslim world.

The communal drinking of *Āb-i-shifā*ʾ was related to both Muslim and Saṁvat (Northern Indian Hindu) calendars held on Fridays, the night of the new moon (*Ćandraat*) and other major festival occasions when a larger congregation was present. The ceremony followed the completion of the formal prayer, called *Duʿā*;[13] among the Nizārī Ismāʿīlīs, individuals lined up behind each other in front of the *pāṭ* and they drank from a small cup into which the *Āb-i-shifā*ʾ had been poured from a larger vessel. The members of the congregation are also given an offering of a sweet food after having completed the ceremony. In the *ginān*s reference is made to this offering and particular emphasis is laid on the symbolism of the five ingredients that are used for making it—milk, sugar, clarified butter, wheat flour and water. Each of these ingredients is said to signify a moral or spiritual trait such as purity, generosity, a spirit of cooperation, moral strenght and spiritual seeking.

There are several aspects of the total ceremony that need to be considered, firstly in their initial context as representing a transition from a Hindu world view to a Muslim one, and secondly in an African context as establishing a continuity and adaptation of past practice. In the context of the larger process of conversion in medieval times from Hinduism to Islam in the community, the ceremony fulfills several important functions. It affirms a notion of purity, but also revises it, through a ritual form that has indigenous Indian roots. In the new and changed order, however, purity and impurity are projected as representing a new order which seeks to integrate a number of castes and relate their allegiance to an external figure—the Shīʿa Ismāʿīlī Imam.[14]

The sources of the water, the well of *zamzam* in Mecca or the sacred places in Karbala, reinforce the symbolic and ritual link with Shīʿa Ismāʿīlī Islam. The *ginān*s also include many references which link the ceremony to Qurʾānic descriptions of the spring of *al-Kauthar*.[15] Classical Ismāʿīlī works include *ṭahāra*, or ritual purity, among the traditional pillars of faith.[16] Thus an overarching frame of Islamic metaphors is used to establish the new religious and social order within which the ritual is seen to have significance. Several other functional characteristics of the ceremony can also be identified as elements that reinforce a new religious and social identity and also consolidate allegiance to an Imam as the pivotal figure of authority, in bonding the followers into a community.

It is however at the level of its esoteric and symbolic significance that the ceremony affords an opportunity for analysing a synthesis between Hindu and Muslim religious experience. This relates in particular to the aspect of transition and liminality at the level of individual religious life that has the most interesting implications in terms of esoteric Hinduism and Islam. As Victor Turner has shown on the basis of his analysis of metaphors in Hindu culture, the fourth stage of life in a Hindu's quest according to the prescriptions of *dharma*, the joining of an *ashram*, represents the antistructural element to the structural closures of caste.[17] Much of *bhaktī* and *sant* poetry also illustrate this. The ceremony of *ghaṭ-pāṭ*, interpreted in its esoteric or *bāṭinī* aspects in Indian Ismāᶜīlism, enables the individual follower to participate in one of the profoundest religious experiences possible. As described in various *ginān*s, the drinking of the sacred water is the equivalent of the experience of unity, when the individual soul embraces the light (*nūr*) of *imāma*. The ritual merges the individual at one level into the new community, at another it frees him from the merely structural or *ẓāhirī* [literally, "exterior"] aspects of ritual and enables him to experience the dimension of *bāṭin*, the interior religion through which his individual quest for spiritual knowledge and understanding is attained.[18]

In its East African context, the ceremony established a continuity with past practice and also incorporated the full range of meanings and experiences already present in its practice. But in addition it became a vehicle for adapting to changed conditions and a means to effecting a degree of social and religious change. The community in East Africa, during the period of its full growth (from 1920 onwards), consisted of groups of Ismāᶜīlīs from many parts of what was then British India. As they sought to establish themselves in a colonial society, they were faced with problems of reorganization, adaptation and establishing structures that reflected the goals of a united, centrally organized religious community. One of the instruments that facilitated this process, as the Ismāᶜīlī Imam of the time sought to realize these goals, was the system of rituals that had linked various community groups under more disparate circumstances in the Subcontinent.[19] The ceremony of *ghaṭ-pāṭ* was made less elaborate by abridging the length of the prayers and recitations accompanying the ritual. In due course when the prayers among Ismāᶜīlīs of Indian origin were made uniform with other Ismāᶜīlīs elsewhere, the *ghaṭ-pāṭ* ceremony was made to blend with it. This also meant that the younger members of the congregation, who may have had difficulty mastering the Khōjki language used earlier, now were allowed to lead the prayers that preceded the ceremony. Prayers could also be led by women, a standard feature in contemporary Ismāᶜīlī practice, but one that only gradually came to be established, paving the way for a greater role for Ismāᶜīlī women not only in religious but eventually also in social life in the community. The *ghaṭ-pāṭ* ceremony is thus a useful ritual for analyzing, diachronically, how patterns of belief and of community organization are interdependent and a significant clue to how a religious community adapts its symbols and concepts in new and unfamiliar situations.

The sketch of the two groups described above is necessarily brief and even impressionistic. An argument could perhaps be made for not treating two such diverse Muslim groups together in one essay. One justification for doing so, however, is to permit a cross-cultural approach and to show some affinities in the way Muslims from different cultural backgrounds interpret and practise their faith. Both groups illustrate the existence of tension that is always present during periods of transition and the desire to affirm their faith, whenever transitional situations create uncertainty and fear. They also reflect the constant need to resolve the ambiguities or even contradictions that occur between past practice and allegiances to new ones. One of the most striking works of fiction written by a modern African Muslim embodies this dilemma in the title of his work, *L'Aventure ambigüe* (Ambiguous Adventure).[20] Such a quest holds equally true for the scholar of African Islam and for Muslims there, as they seek resolution in the face of increasing ambiguity.

NOTES

1 Camara Laye, *L'Enfant Noir*, trans. as *The Dark Child* (New York: The Noonday Press, 1954).

2 For the *ginān*s and a history of the Nizārī Ismāʿīlis, see Azim Nanji, *The Nizārī Ismāʿīlī Tradition in the Indo-Pakistan Subcontinent* (New York: Caravan Books, 1978).

3 This assumption is reflected in some of the more general studies on African Islam, such as those of J. Trimingham and more specifically focused works on legal aspects, such as those of J. N. Anderson. Useful correctives are addressed in D. F. Eickleman's essay appearing in this volume where the field of Islamic Studies is surveyed. For African contexts see, J. R. Willis, "The Historiography of Islam in Africa: The Last Decade", *African Studies Review*, 14/3, (1971): 403-424; and Robin Horton, "African Conversion", *Africa* 41 (1971): 85-108. For a general bibliography, see P. Ojori, *Islam in Africa South of the Sahara* (Nendeln, Holland, KTO Press, 1977).

4 Clifford Geertz, *Islam Observed* (Chicago, University of Chicago Press, 1968), p. 14.

5 This revised view is outlined in F. A. Isambert, "Religion Populaire, Sociologie, Histoire et Folklore," *Archives de sciences sociales des religions*, 43/2 (1977): p. 161-84. For a survey of developments on the subject in North America, see Peter Williams, *Popular Religion in America* (Englewood Cliffs, N.J.: Prentice-Hall, 1980).

6 The recent publications resulting from a series of conferences related to the Aga Khan Award for Architecture have done much to highlight this. See in particular, *Architecture as Symbol and Self-Identity, Proceedings of Seminar Four* (Philadelphia; The Aga Khan Awards, 1980).

7 Laye, *The Dark Child*, p. 19.

8 *Dark Child*, p. 109.

9 *Dark Child*, p. 113.

10 For the ceremony and the references to it in the *ginān*s, see my *Nizārī Ismāʿīlī Tradition*, p. 105.

11 Literally, "houses of assembly", centers of communal religious and social activity among the Nizārī Ismāʿīlis.

12 The notion of healing is to be understood in a "holistic" sense. It is not certain when the Persian term started to be used interchangeably with *ghāṭ-pāṭ* for the ceremony. The symbolism of water and healing reflects interesting correlations with Hindu ideas of the role of water (bathing tanks attached to temples, the role of sacred pilgrimage sites along the Ganges and other rivers) in bodily and spiritual purification.

13 For this form of prayer and its origins, see *The Nizārī Ismāʿīlī Tradition*, pp. 24-25.

14 *Nizārī Ismāʿīlī*, pp. 105 ff. I am also grateful to Layla McKnight of Harvard University for sharing her insights about the ceremony based on her paper, "Charisma, Ritual and

Change: An Ismaili Example," (presented to the Centre for Middle Eastern Studies, Harvard University, 1979).

15 Sūra 108 of the Qurʾān.

16 See for instance, al-Qāḍī al-Nuʿmān, *Daʿāʾim al-Islām*, ed., A. A. Fyzee (Cairo: Dar al-Maʿārif, 1951), vol. 1.

17 Victor Turner, "Metaphors of Anti-Structure in Religious Culture" in *Changing Perspectives in the Scientific Study of Religion*, ed. A. W. Eister, (New York: John Wiley and Sons, 1974), pp. 63-84.

18 *The Nizārī Ismāʿīlī Tradition*, pp. 120 ff.

19 I have drawn the material for East Africa partly from field work done among the Nizārī Ismāʿīlis there and from the work of Aziz Esmail, *Satpanth Ismaʿilism and Modern Changes Within it with Reference to East Africa* (diss., University of Edinburgh, 1972).

20 Hamidou Kane, *L'Aventure Ambigüe*, trans. into English as *Ambiguous Adventure* (New York, Macmillan Publishing Co., 1969).

Contributions to Asian Studies, Vol. XVII

The Popular Appeal of the Prophetic Paradigm in West Africa

MARILYN ROBINSON WALDMAN
The Ohio State University, Columbus, Ohio, U.S.A.

THE DEVELOPMENT of paradigmatic descriptions of certain types of behavior is well known to students of historical writing. Frank Barlow in his book *Edward the Confessor* gives the example of a description of Edward's death actually based on stylized descriptions of the death of St. Audemer.[1] Such paradigms become so powerful that the historian begins to think, "If he didn't die that way, he should have."

The presence of a powerful paradigm for behavior, in this case of prophet or messenger figure, in Nile-to-Oxus cultures, from Biblical times into Islamic ones, allows us to explore in depth how paradigmatic description functions. By the time of Ibn Isḥāq's biography of Muhammad (Ibn Isḥāq died 767), a paradigm for describing prophetic lives seems already to have been well established. Drawing on Ibn Isḥāq himself, from Biblical material as presented in Abraham Heschel's *The Prophets*, and from information on the life of Zoroaster, we can describe the paradigm in terms of five stages:[2] 1. a to-some-extent ominous infancy, childhood, and/or youth, spent in close association with conventional spiritual and religious norms and also in experimentation with unconventional ones; 2. a sudden, strongly resisted call to Messengership, while in a state of ritual purity and/or a sacred or sacralized place, often at the age of forty; 3. initial preaching among one's own, met by suspicion, resentment, and perhaps outright hostility, producing a small but devoted core of followers; 4. emigration to a new and more receptive environment and gradual development of a larger following, often without abandoning the conventional religion entirely; 5. development of a socio-political community or conversion of and alliance with an existing political power to achieve the same end.

This paradigm can be applied, with slight adjustments, to figures as far apart as Zoroaster and Paul, or Martin Luther and Joseph Smith; once established in the Islamic world, it spreads widely.[3] Using Zoroaster as an example, we can observe his training for the Aryan priesthood combined with possible mystical exercises; his call at the age of forty while bathing to purify himself for sacrifice; his anxiety and reluctance to go with the angel who summoned him to Ahura Mazda; his rejection in his own land and emigration to that of a neighboring king whom he converted and who organized his state around Zoroaster's teachings; and his marrying three times to fulfill the conditions of conventional priesthood, even after he had begun to preach the new message.[4]

Muhammad's youth, as well as his mother's pregnancy, were filled with omens. Though deeply involved in the conventional religion of his day, through his clan's role in the pilgrimage to the Kaᶜba, he also practised meditation more common to various hermit figures. He received his call at forty, while in a state of self-induced purification and in a place made sacred by God, refusing the call thrice as did Moses at the burning bush. His initial preaching produced largely resentment among his own and resulted in his *hijra* to a more hospitable environment, from which he built a socio-political community. Apparently even during his early preaching of the new message in Mecca, he continued to participate to some extent in the pagan *ḥajj*.

The presence of paradigmatic explanation raises interestingly complex questions: Once a paradigm is established, how flexible or rigid is it? Does any behavior by a person to whom it might apply get molded into the paradigm? Or do persons who want to be recognized as prophets mold their behavior to fit the legitimating paradigm held by their intended followers?[5] And, finally, does the audience perceive the behavior of an actor in ways that maximize its correspondence to their prefigured expectations?

Two things are clear in the Islamic case: a paradigm that becomes strongly attached to one figure can be applied to or by another figure (even if he is not a prophet per se but rather a reformer), or it can be adjusted to a new situation. An example of the former is Ibn Tūmart, the twelfth-century North African Muwahhid reformer who received his "call" at forty, made a *hijra*, and divided his followers into *anṣār* and *muhājirūn*, the terms for the Medinan "Helpers" and Meccan "Emigrants" respectively. An example of the latter possibility is the "Mantle Poem" of al-Buṣīrī (b. 1212), in which the fairly sober and unadorned picture of Muhammad from the tradition of Ibn Isḥāq is embellished with a miraculous layer suitable for a Muslim and Christian audience in the era of the Crusades.

A less-well-known African case is Usuman dan Fodio, the Fulani *mujāhid* in Hausaland in the early nineteenth century. As described by his brother Abdallāh in the *Tazyīn al-waraqāt* and numerous other works, Usuman spent his youth as a traditional *mallam* (Arabic *muᶜallim*) working for the Sarki (ruler) of Gobir, compromising with the conventional syncretistic Islam of the court but also dabbling in the more severe reform tradition of some of his teachers. He apparently waited until he was forty to begin his public preaching of the new dispensation. After escaping a variously described assassination attempt, he, with a small band of loyal followers, made his *hijra*; organized a Hausa-wide movement of revolt under the label of *jihād*; and founded a new politico-religious state, organized along early ᶜAbbāsid administrative lines, but in the spirit of the early Islam of Muhammad's own *umma*.[6] In his own writings, Usuman sees Muhammad's situation as directly analogous to his.[7]

Knowing all of this, I began to wonder, if Abdallāh writes about his brother the way Ibn Isḥāq wrote about Muhammad, how would he write about Muhammad himself? It was my good fortune some years ago to happen upon a reference to an undated work by Abdallāh entitled *Ḍiyāʾ ūlīʾ l-amr wa l-mujāhidīn fī siyar al-nabī wa l-khulafāʾ al-rāshidīn.*[8] Abdallāh was one of the most prolific *jihād* authors, with more than seventy-five works attributed to him.[9] This manuscript was number 193 of the Gironcourt Mission, copied by eight African copyists in the Gao region in 1912 and housed in the Bibliothèque Nationale as number 5634. It is 417 folios long, divided into a *muqaddima* [prologue]; five *bāb*s [chapters] on Muhammad, the first four caliphs and ʿUmar ibn ʿAbd al-ʿAzīz; and a *khātima* [epilogue]. It has to have been written between the declaration of the *jihād* in 1804 and Abdallah's death in 1828. It was probably, from internal evidence, written after 1810, when the Fulani Amīr al-Muʾminīn adopted the title of *khalīfa* as well. I say this because the *muqaddima* contains a very interesting discussion, based on quotations from the five caliphs mentioned above, of the relationship between *mulk* and *khilāfa* (i.e., between political power and Muslim concepts of rule), an issue that surfaced right before the *jihād* was declared but that really began to simmer in the years after 1810.

The first forty-five folios of the manuscript are the *muqaddima*; the next 179, about Muhammad. It is clear from a study of the text that Abdallāh's account of Muhammad, as is evidenced even by the text's title, has a focus suited to the Hausa situation. Abdallāh's emphasis is on rule and rulership, and on the expansion thereof by military and diplomatic activity of various kinds. As such, the work adheres more to the *maghāzī* tradition of the early Muslim wars than to that of the *sīra* or prophetic biography. It is essentially a narrative of Muhammad's and many other related figures' raiding parties, under the rubric *ghazwa* or *sarīya.* Even the conquest of Mecca is referred to as the *ghazwa* of the conquest of Mecca (fol. 180). Descriptions of how Muhammad became a Messenger of God, what nonmilitary functions that entailed, how he died—are all kept to a bare minimum.

Within this long succession of numerous *ghazwa*s and *sarīya*s, Abdallāh's preoccupation with ruler-subordinate relationships is notable, especially when one recalls how problematic this relationship was in the Hausa *jihād.* The pattern of relationships and activities that Abdallāh presents is somewhat decentralized, with Muhammad constantly delegating authority for raids to others. He is even said to have sent banners (*liwāʾ*) as tokens of authority (e.g., fol. 171): the sending of banners was an essential ritual of delegation in Usuman's *jihād*, and a problematic one sometimes involving false claims.

Especially in his account of the early years in Medina after the Hijra, Abdallāh dwells on the tensions between *muhājirūn* and *anṣār* and on Muhammad's need to reconcile their interests in such a way as to boost the morale of the *anṣār.* Once again, one must note Usuman's division of his followers into *muhājirūn* and *anṣār* and his difficulties in welding them together, which were made more serious by the ethnic differences among them. One issue that Abdallāh describes as particularly troublesome for Muhammad was the division of booty after a raid and the handling of wealth in general—also two key issues for Usuman.

Of particular note in the Hausa context is Abdallāh's unusually detailed specificity as to clan and tribe, and his emphasis on Muhammad's relationship with the tribes and his corresponding deemphasis of his relationship with the Meccan Quraysh. For Usuman, once again, the status and relationships of the various clans among the Fulani were as much of a problem as were the Bedouin for Muhammad.

Finally, we come to Abdallāh's constant and fairly loose application of the words *kuffār* and *mushrikūn* to Muhammad's enemies and his relatively infrequent use of more subtle Qurʾānic designations like *munāfiqūn* "hypocrites." It should be remembered that these two words were *the* critical labels used by Usuman and his cohorts to justify their campaigns against not only pagans but self-proclaimed Muslims as well. Once again, Abdallāh finds salient in Muhammad's career a feature which has been central in his brother's.

In returning now to our original questions about the power of leadership paradigms, we find that we have discovered from this brief textual analysis how truly circular is the relationship among paradigm, experience, and description. Just as one paradigm of Muhammad governed, in some ways, Usuman's career, Usuman's career and the peculiarities of his evolving situation subtly (and sometimes not so subtly) skewed his brother's account of Muhammad's paradigm, such that his Messengership became subordinated to his status as Commander and Coordinator of a tribal military expansion much like Usuman's movement. But then the classical paradigm developed by Ibn Isḥāq was also created in a historical and cultural context and was more likely to appeal to his partially Christian and Jewish, rather than tribal, audience.

The analysis of such circularity of relationship between symbol and society is already generating great interest among students of religion.[10] Our look at one African case has shown that the study of paradigmatic descriptions of prophetic and prophet-like behavior is exciting though it requires a much more expanded study of biographical literature.

NOTES

1 Frank Barlow, *Edward the Confessor* (Berkeley: University of California Press, 1970), chap. 1.

2 Abraham Heschel, *The Prophets* (New York: Harper and Row, 1969); Mary Boyce, *A History of Zoroastrianism* (Leiden: Brill, 1975), vol. 1, chap. 1); Muhammad ibn Isḥāq, trans. Alfred Guillaume, *The Life of Muhammad* (Lahore: Oxford University Press, 1955). This paradigm is essential to the monotheistic pattern of concepts, emphasizing as it does the continuing humanness and worldliness of God's chosen servants, even after they are elevated to Messengership.

3 Jesus, the central Christian messenger, is obviously described in the Gospels in terms of another paradigm—that of the dying and living god. One wonders, though, whether the Messenger paradigm might have at some point been replaced with the other one.

4 Boyce, *History of Zoroastrianism*, vol. 1, chap. 1.
5 See and compare the interesting article by Stanley and Inge Hoffman, "The Will to Grandeur: de Gaulle as Political Artist," *Daedalus* (1968): 829-87.
6 ᶜAbdallāh b. Fūdī, trans. M. Hiskett, *Tazyīn al-waraqāt* (Ibadan: Ibadan University Press, 1963).
7 Marilyn Robinson Waldman, "The Fulani *Jihād*: A Reassessment," *Journal of African History* 6 (1965): 333-55.
8 Georges Vajda, "Contribution à la connaissance de la littérature arabe en Afrique occidentale," *Journal de la société des africanistes* 19 (1949-50): 233.
9 W. E. N. Kensdale, "Field Notes on the Arabic Literature of the Western Sudan," *Journal of the Royal Asiatic Society* pts. 1-2 (1956): 78-80.
10 Clifford Geertz, "Religion as a Cultural System," in *The Interpretation of Cultures* (New York: Basic Books, 1973), 87-125.

CONTRIBUTORS

RICHARD M. EATON is associate professor of Oriental Studies, University of Arizona at Tucson. His Ph.D. in History is from the University of Wisconsin. He is the author of *Sufis of Bijapur, 1300-1700: Social Roles of Sufis in Medieval India* (Princeton University Press, 1978). In 1979-80 he was a fellow at the National Humanities Center in North Carolina where he conducted research on conversion in India. In 1981-82 he conducted further research in India and Bangladesh on related topics.

DALE F. EICKELMAN is associate professor of Anthropology at New York University. He holds a M.A. in Islamic Studies from McGill University, and a M.A. and Ph.D. (1971) in Anthropology from the University of Chicago. He is the author of *Moroccan Islam: Tradition and Society in a Pilgrimage Center* (University of Texas Press, 1976) and *The Middle East: An Anthropological Approach* (Prentice-Hall, 1981).

RAPHAEL ISRAELI is lecturer in Chinese History and Islamic Civilization at Hebrew University in Jerusalem. His Ph.D. in History is from the University of California at Berkeley. His many writings include works on Islam in Asia, and Middle Eastern affairs: he is the author of *Muslims in China* (Amazon Press, 1980) and the editor of *Islam in the Asian Environment* (Amazon Press, forthcoming).

JIN YIJIU is professor of Islamic Studies at the Institute for Research on World Religions, a part of the Chinese Academy of Social Sciences, Beijing, Peoples Republic of China. Prof. Jin is presently engaged in a project in Qurʾānic studies at the Institute to translate and publish an edition of the Qurʾān in Mandarin.

BRUCE B. LAWRENCE is professor in the Department of Religion, Duke University. His Ph.D. in Near Eastern studies is from Yale University. Among his writings are *Shahrastani on the Indian Religions* (Mouton, 1976) and *Notes from a Distant Flute* (Great Eastern, 1979). He is a member of the South Asia Council of the Association of Asian Studies and on the editorial boards of *Journal of South Asian Literature* and *Encyclopaedia Iranica.*

RICHARD C. MARTIN is associate professor of Religious Studies at Arizona State University, Tempe, Arizona. His Ph.D. in Near Eastern Languages and Literature is from New York University. He is the author of *Islam: A Cultural Prespective* (Prentice-Hall, 1981) and the editor of *Islam and the History of Religions*: Prespectives on the Study of a Religious Tradition (Berkeley Religious Studies Series, 1983). He is on the editorial board of *Journal of the American Academy of Religions.*

BARBARA DALY METCALF is assistant professor of South Asian Regional Studies at the University of Pennsylvania. Her Ph.D. in Near Eastern Studies is from the University of California at Berkeley. Her book, *Islamic Revival in Nineteenth-Century India* will be published by Princeton University Press.

AZIM NANJI is associate professor of Religious Studies and chairperson of the Department of Humanities, Oklahoma State University at Stillwater, Oklahome. His Ph.D. is from Harvard University. He is the author of *The Nizari Ismaʿili Tradition in the Indo-Pakistani Subcontinent* (Caravan Books, 1978). In 1981-82 he was on leave to conduct research on Ismaʿili Studies.

ANNEMARIE SCHIMMEL is professor of Indo-Muslim Culture at Harvard University. She holds several degrees, including a D.Phil. from Berlin. She is President of the International Association for the History of Religions and a member of numerous professional associations and learned societies, including foreign member of the Royal Dutch Academy of Sciences. Among her many books and articles are *Islam in the Indian Subcontinent* (1980) and *Mystical Dimensions of Islam* (University of North Carolina Press, 1975).

Marilyn R. Waldman is associate professor of History and Chair of the Division of Comparative Studies, Ohio State University at Columbus. Her Ph.D. in History from the University of Chicago was in Middle Eastern Civilizations and History of Religion. Among her publications is *Toward a Theory of Historical Narrative: A Case Study of Perso-Islamicate Historiography* (Ohio State University Press, 1980), and (with William McNeill) *The Islamic World* (Oxford University Press, 1974).

INDEX